CW00922891

Knitting for special effect

Knitting for special effect

Debby Robinson

LITTLE, BROWN AND COMPANY
BOSTON · TORONTO · LONDON

DEDICATION

To Butch the cat

ACKNOWLEDGEMENTS

The photographs in *Knitting for Special Effect* were shot at Southside House, Wimbledon Common, London and I would like to give very special thanks to John and Roy for all their very good-humoured assistance and to Major Munthe for graciously allowing us to use his home which is now administered by the Pennington-Mellor Charity Trust. Guided tours of the house are possible at certain times. Details may be obtained by telephoning 081-946 7643.
I would also like to thank the creative team:

Photography Christopher Bissell
Art Direction Christopher Stevenson
Hair and Make-up Joanne Harber
Illustrations Kate Simunek

Lastly, many thanks to all the suppliers mentioned at the back of the book and most importantly to all my long-suffering knitters without whom none of this would have been possible.

First published in Great Britain in 1990 by
Little, Brown and Company (UK) Limited
Beacon House, 30 North End Road, London W14 0SH

ISBN 0–316–75147–2

A CIP Catalogue Record for this book
is available from the British Library

Designed by Janet James
Technical Editor Jackie Owen

10 9 8 7 6 5 4 3 2 1

Typeset by DP Photosetting, Aylesbury, Bucks
Printed and bound in Spain
by Printer Barcelona

ABBREVIATIONS/GLOSSARY

alt	alternate(ly)
aran wool	fisherman yarn (knitted worsted-weight)
beg	begin(ning)
b	(as in 'K1 b') into back
cast off	bind off
CB	cable back
CF	cable front
CN	cable needle
cm	centimetre(s)
cont	continue/ continuing
dc	double crochet (US single crochet)
dec	decrease/ decreasing
DK	double knitting (US slightly finer than knitting worsted – see Buying Yarn page 96)
inc	increase/ increasing
k	knit
LH	left hand
M1	make one by lifting strand between sts and knitting into the back of it
patt	pattern
p	purl
psso	pass slipped stitch over
rep	repeat
revers	lapels
rev stst	reverse st st
RH	right hand
RS	right side
sl	slip
st(s)	stitch(s)
st st	stocking stitch (US stockinette stitch)
studs	snaps
Swiss darning	duplicate stitch embroidery
tbl	through back of loop(s)
tension	gauge
tog	together
tr	treble crochet (US double crochet)
WS	wrong side
yo	yarn over needle
yrn	yarn round needle (US a yarn – over worked between a knit and a purl stitch)

NOTE ON SIZING

To check the size of a pattern, please refer to the diagrams showing the measurements of the various pattern pieces. If there are two sizes, they will be given thus: 51/54cm (20/21¼in). The required yarn is given as 600/650g – the smaller size requires 600g, the larger 650g.

c o n t e n t s

foreword

Over the many years that I have been designing and producing hand knits, my first consideration has always been the technical feasibility of each pattern. In other words, the knitter's skills come first and foremost, rather than creating an idea strictly on the sketch-pad which then becomes a nightmare once it has been translated to the knitting needle.

By working closely with my knitters, I like to feel that I have also developed a style of pattern writing which, while being clear and concise, also gives as much guidance as is possible, especially when it comes to the finishing instructions. In addition, the patterns which require specific decorative techniques, such as fringes or tassles, are accompanied by easy-to-follow diagrams.

In *Knitting for Special Effect* I have included designs for every level of knitting ability and so I hope the collection contains something for everybody. A great many of the patterns use nothing more complicated than stocking stitch and basic rib, but with the addition of a few clever finishing touches, styles with a very special look are created.

Even the plainest of sweaters can be transformed with a scattering of pearls or gem stones and many of the suggestions within this collection are meant as starting points for your own imagination. Browse around bead shops, take embroidery ideas from any source that inspires you – the possibilities are endless.

Debby Robinson
London April 1990

An exotic cropped evening top with golden swirls knitted into yoke and border. Finishing touches are added with gold coins, tassles and braid.

turkish . . *delight*

NEEDLES

One pair each 3.75mm and 3.25mm needles.

TENSION

Measured over st st, using 3.75mm needles:
24 sts = 10cm.

MATERIALS

Jaeger Gauguin in Venetian: 250g
Twilley's Doublegold in gold: 100g.
Coins (or beads): 20.

BACK AND FRONT

(Worked identically)
Using 3.75mm needles and Venetian, cast on 114 sts. Work in st st for 11cm.

Shape armhole and neck

Row 1: Cast off 3 sts, work to end.
Row 2: Cast off 3 sts, work 39 sts, cast off 30, work to end. Cont with this set of sts, leaving others on a holder. Dec 1 st at armhole edge on next and every alt row throughout whilst at the neck edge dec 1 st every row for 11 rows and then dec 1 st at this edge on every alt row, as for armhole edge, until 2 sts remain, work 2 tog and fasten off. Return to held sts, join yarn in at neck edge and work to match the first side.

SLEEVES

Using 3.25mm needles and Venetian, cast on 88 sts and knit the first, WS row. Change to gold and knit 3 rows. Change to Venetian and 3.75mm needles, purl the next row and cont in st st. When sleeve measures 4cm:

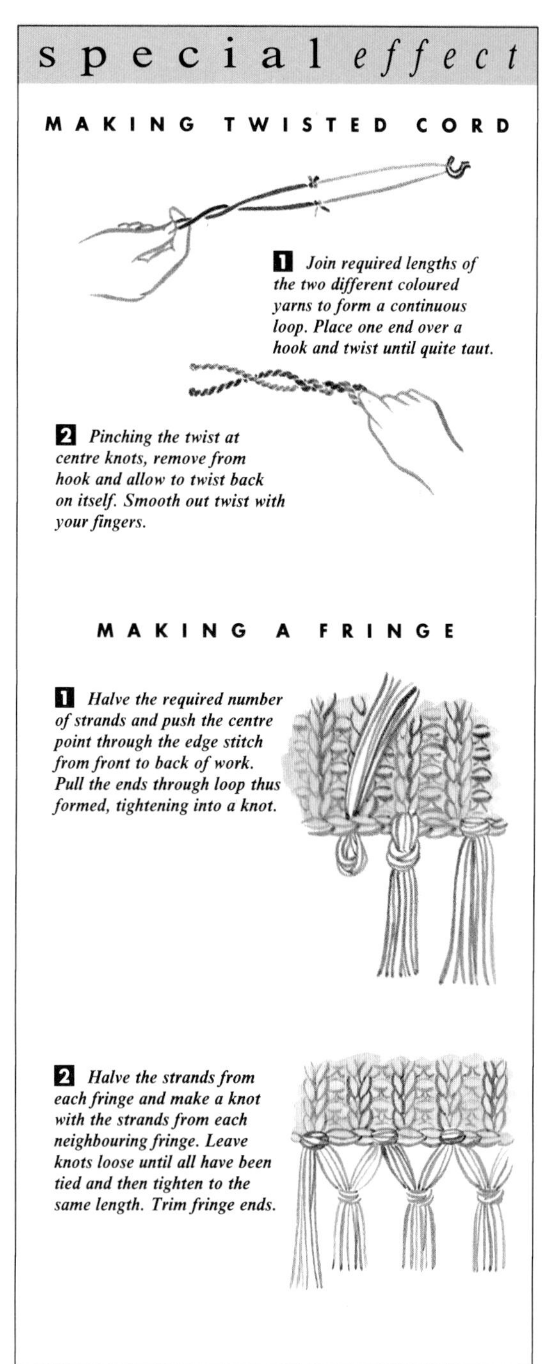

Shape sleeve head

Cast off 3 sts at beg of next 2 rows. Now dec 1 st each end of next and every following alt row until 50 sts remain. Cast off loosely.

BORDER

Using 3.75mm needles and Venetian, cast on 21 sts and work from graph, starting on a WS row and slipping the first st on every RS row. The main motif is worked in st st whilst the 2 st border is in garter st. Rep the graph 16 times in all. Cast off.

YOKE

As for border but working an extra 2 rows thus: Purl 12 sts, turn and k to end. Rep these 18 rows 16 times in all. Cast off.

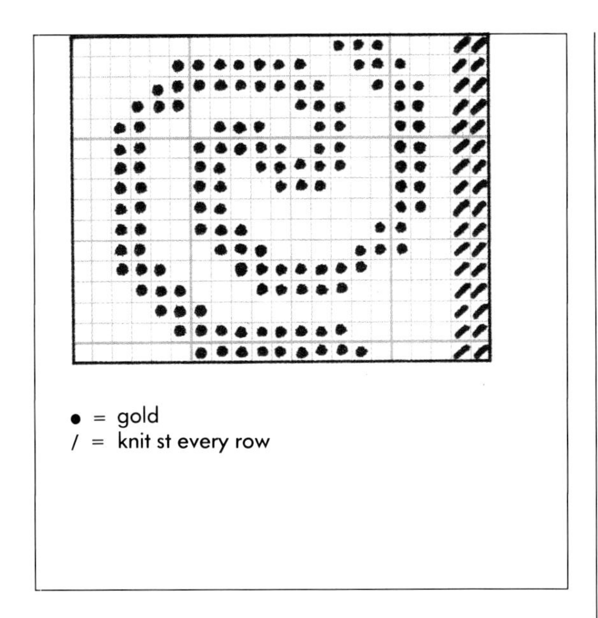

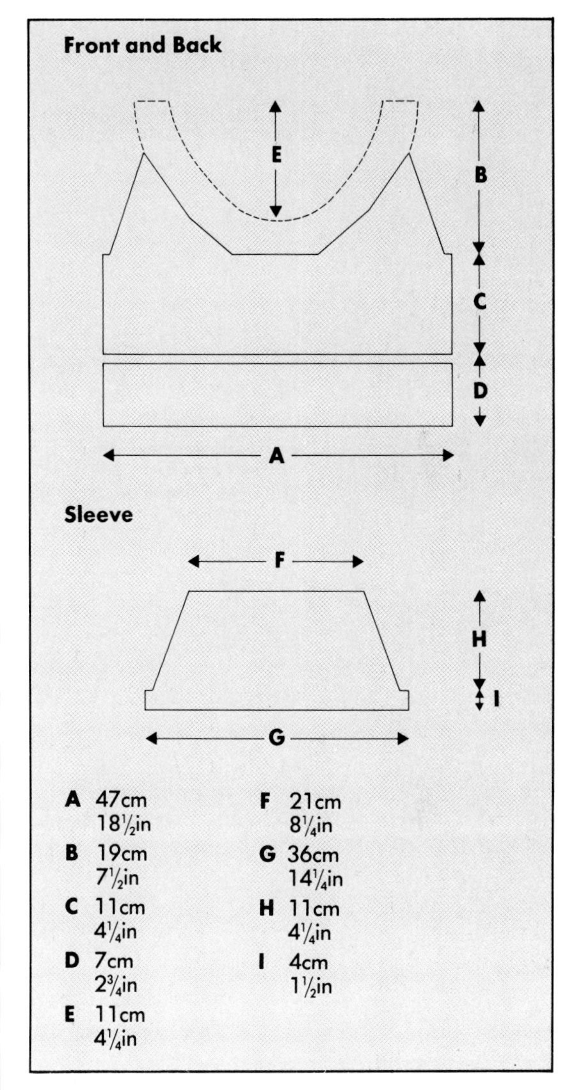

MAKING UP

Join all seams with flat seams. Join sleeves to armholes first and then work sleeve and side seams.

Join the cast on and cast off edges of border and attach it around the hemline with the garter st border to the bottom.

Join the edges of the yoke similarly and join this to body with the garter st border forming the neck edge.

To make a braid cut an approx 3 metre length of each colour yarn. Join and twist (as shown in diagrams opposite). Work two braids and attach one around the line of the yoke seam and the other around the line of the border seam. Slip stitch these into position using a piece of main colour yarn which has been divided into two strands. To neaten the ends of the braid carefully push them through to the wrong side of work and secure there.

To make fringes, cut approx 35cm lengths of main colour yarn (winding yarn around a book of suitable size is the best way of quickly cutting numerous identical lengths), and using 7 lengths per fringe knot around hem line as shown in diagrams opposite.

Finally add gold coins or beads in between fringes as shown in close up.

A stylish wool cardigan with twisting vine motifs picked out in chenille to create a decorative and striking 'flocked' effect.

victorian ... *vines*

NEEDLES

One pair each 4mm and 3.75mm.

TENSION

Measured over st st, using 4mm needles:
22 sts = 10cm.
NB The chenille yarn is thicker than the DK to exaggerate the 'flocked' effect. Any unevenness will press out.
The DK wool is used throughout, being carried at the back of the chenille pattern areas and woven in every 3/4 sts.

MATERIALS

Rowan Designer DK in colour no 657: 600/650g.
Rowan Chenille in 'Teak': 100g.
10 buttons.

RIGHT FRONT

Using 3.75mm needles, cast on 64/68 sts.
Row 1 RS: * K2, p2, rep from * to end.
Keep rep this row to form double rib for 6cm. Change to 4mm needles and cont in st st, working from the graph, shaping as shown.

LEFT FRONT

As for right front, reversing out the shapings and pattern, starting rib p2, k2.
NB Now block both fronts so that they lie quite flat (see diagram on page 72 for blocking).

BACK

Using 3.75mm needles, cast on 136/144 sts. Work in double rib for 6cm. Change to 4mm needles and cont

in st st, shaping armholes and shoulders to match the fronts. Finally casting off 40/42 back neck sts.

SLEEVES

Using 3.75mm needles, cast on 48/52 sts and work in double rib as for back for 6cm. Now cont in st st, inc into every 8th st across the first row (54/58 sts). Change to 4mm needles working from the sleeve graph followed by plain st st and inc 1 st each end of next and every following 4th row until there are 106 sts. Work straight until sleeve measures 43/45cm. Cast off loosely.

LEFT BAND AND COLLAR

First join both shoulder seams tog with a narrow backstitch.
Using 3.75mm needles, cast on 12 sts and work in double rib as for left front (i.e. so that the band will cont in rib patt when attached). When band is long enough to reach the start of the neck shaping on the front:

Shape collar
Next RS row: inc into first st, rib to end. Cont inc 1 st at this edge on every 4th row, working new sts into double rib as you go, until you have 36 sts on the needle. Now work straight until it is long enough to

reach the dead centre of the back neck. Cast off knitwise.
Mark 10 button positions equally spaced between the start of collar shaping and a point 1cm up from the hem.

RIGHT BAND AND COLLAR

Using 3.75mm needles, cast on 12 sts. Work in double rib as for right front.
Cont as for left band but reversing out shapings and working buttonholes on RS rows to correspond with button markers, thus:
Buttonhole row: K2, p2, k1, cast off next 2 sts, rib to end.
Next row: Rib, casting on 2 sts immediately above those cast off on previous row.

MAKING UP

Open out body and set sleeves into the armholes to form a 'T'. Join with a flat seam. Only then join the sleeve and side seams with a flat seam.

Join the centre back neck seam of the collar with a flat seam. Carefully pin the bands to the fronts so that they are evenly distributed, remembering that it is the shaped edges which are joined to one another. Attach with a flat seam.

Attach buttons.

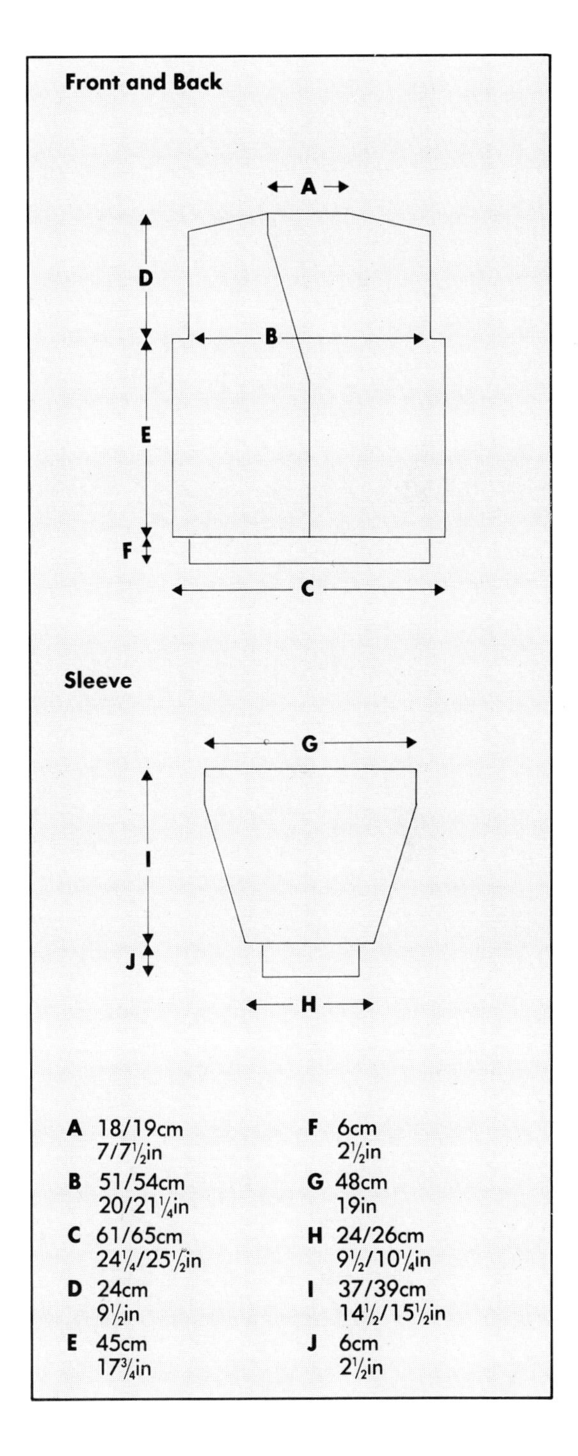

v i c t o r i a n

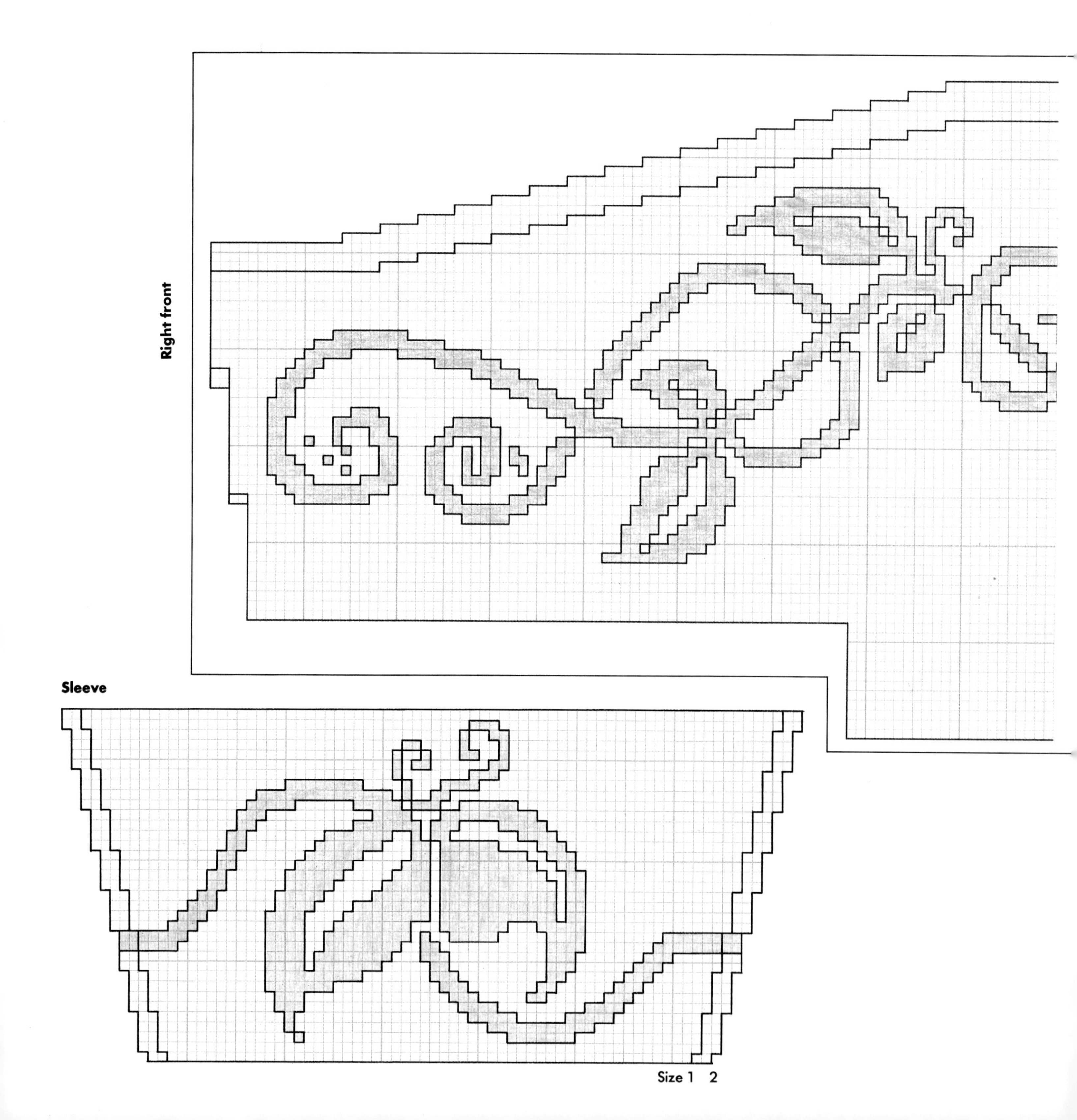

Size 1 2

An elegant little top, with a romantic flavour, knitted from side to side in matt cotton and trimmed with tassles.

spanish ...bolero

NEEDLES

First size: One pair each 3.75mm and 4mm.
Second size: One pair each 3.75, 4mm and 4.5mm.

TENSION

Since this bolero is knitted sideways, using the graph, the sizing is ruled by the difference in tensions. Always check your tension before starting a garment.
Measured over st st:
Size 1: Using 4mm needles: 20 sts = 10cm.
Size 2: Using 4.5mm needles: 19 sts = 10cm.

MATERIALS

Rowan Handknit DK Cotton:
Colourway 1: 150g of Cherry (A), 400g of Black (B).
Colourway 2: 150g of Wheat (A), 400g of Nut (B).
NB Use separate balls of yarn for each area of colour unless you have a very small gap where the colour not in use may be carried loosely at the back of the work, weaving in every 4 sts or so.

RIGHT BACK AND FRONT

(Starting at right cuff). Using 3.75/4mm needles and A, cast on 44 sts and work in garter st (k every row), for 10 rows, the first row being a WS row. Now change to 4/4.5mm needles and work colour pattern from graph, keeping in st st throughout. **NB** Work all shapings 2 sts in from the edge and in the following ways.

Incs:
Work 2 sts, now work into the next st on the row below and then work into the st itself.

Single Decs:
At beg of a K row: K2, k2 tog tbl.
At end of a K row: K to last 4 sts, k2 tog, k2.
At beg of a P row: P2, p2 tog.
At end of a P row: P to last 3 sts, sl last worked st back on to LH needle, lift the next st on LH needle over it and then sl the result back to the RH needle, p2.

s p a n i s h

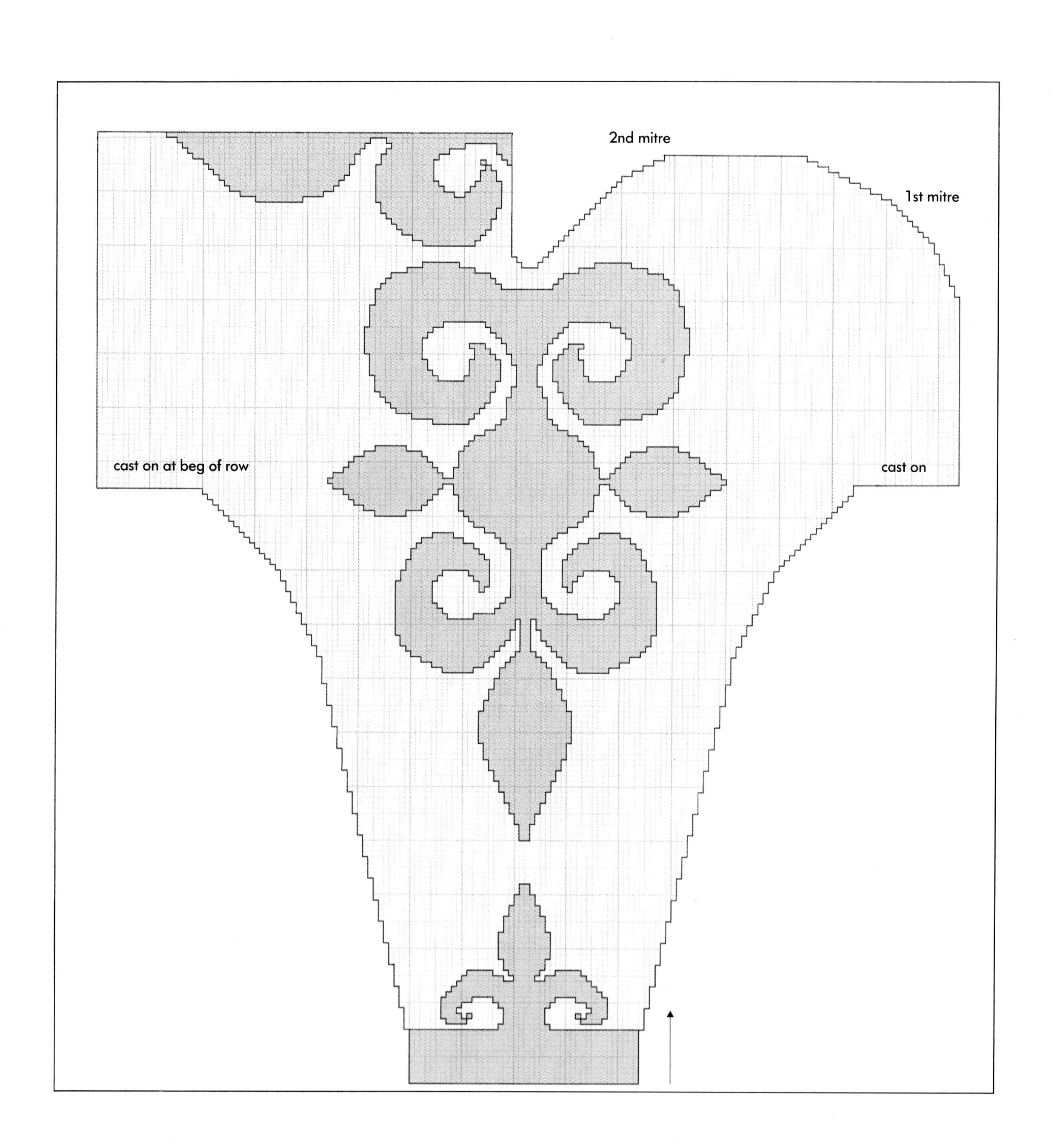

Double Decs:
At beg of a K row: K2, k2 tog tbl, k1, k2 tog tbl.
At end of a K row: K to last 7 sts, k2 tog, k1, k2 tog, k2.
At beg of a P row: P2, p2 tog, p1, p2 tog.
At end of P row: P to last 7 sts, * sl the last worked st back on to the LH needle, lift the next st on the LH needle over it and then slip the result back to the RH needle *, p1, rep from * to *, p2.
When the graph is complete, leave sts on a spare needle.

LEFT BACK AND FRONT

Work the mirror image of the first side so that the first row will be a RS row. When complete knit the two pieces tog on the inside of work to form the centre back seam.

RIGHT BAND

First press the fronts.
Using 3.75mm needles and B, cast on 6 sts and work in garter st until it is long enough to reach from the centre back seam to the first mitre point when very slightly stretched (carefully pin band to work as you go).

Work mitre
Next RS row: K4, turn and k to end.
Row 3 and 4: K2, turn and k to end.
Now cont straight until 2nd mitre point and work another mitre in the same way. Cont straight until band reaches centre back seam. Cast off.

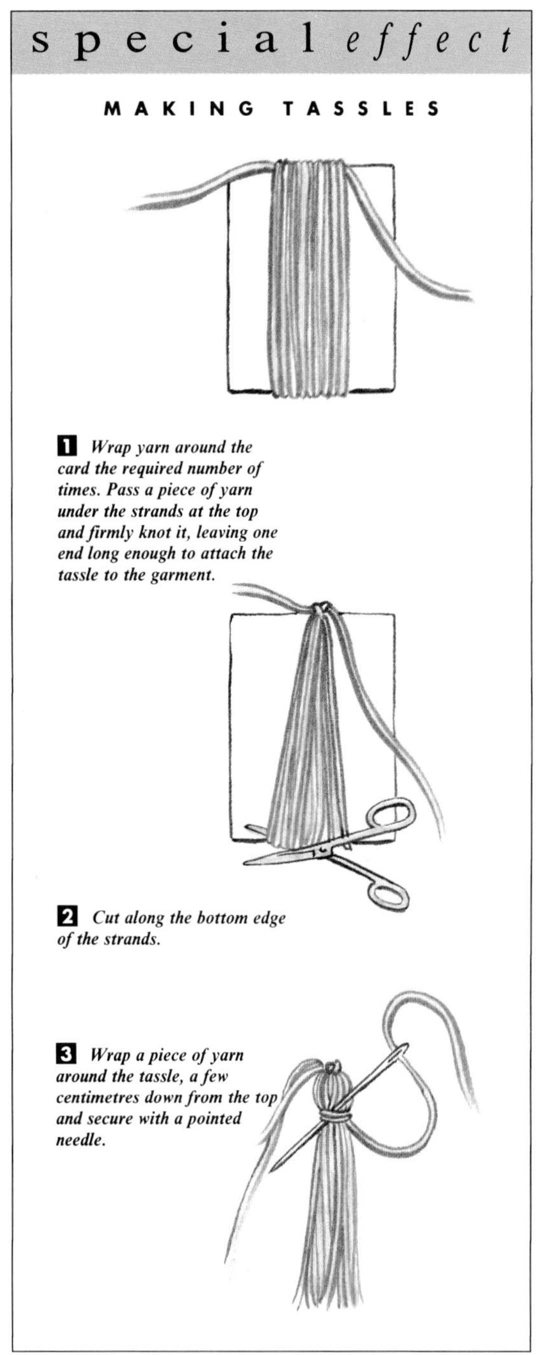

special *effect*

MAKING TASSLES

1 *Wrap yarn around the card the required number of times. Pass a piece of yarn under the strands at the top and firmly knot it, leaving one end long enough to attach the tassle to the garment.*

2 *Cut along the bottom edge of the strands.*

3 *Wrap a piece of yarn around the tassle, a few centimetres down from the top and secure with a pointed needle.*

LEFT BAND

Work as for left band, working mitres on WS rows. When band reaches centre back neck when very slightly stretched, cast off.

MAKING UP

Join side and sleeves seam with a flat seam.

Join cast on edge to cast on edge, cast off to cast off on bands. Attach with a flat seam, taking great care to distribute them evenly and ease them around the curves of the fronts.

Make 6 tassles, as illustrated left, using a piece of card approx 10cm deep and wrapping the yarn right around the card 10 times. Attach to the bolero as shown in photographs.

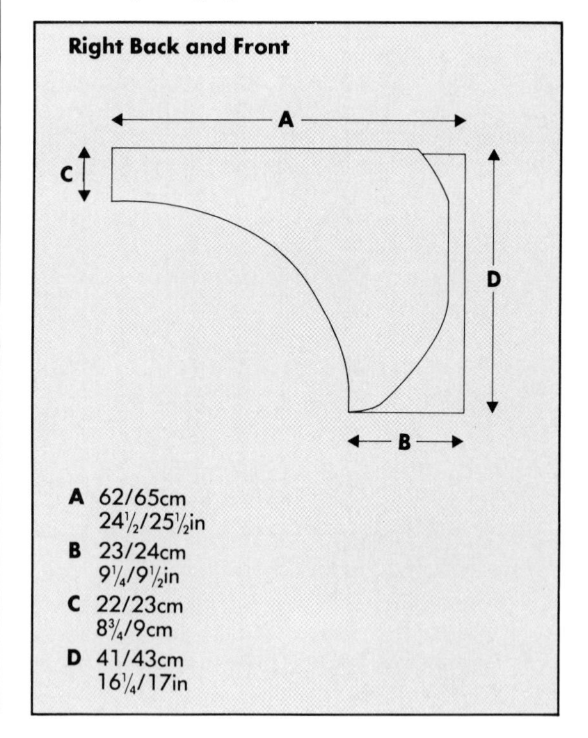

A glamorous mock leather jacket in smooth cotton, which is smartly finished with pockets, studs and zip just like the real thing.

black . . *leather*

NEEDLES

One pair each 3.25mm and 3mm.

TENSION

Measured over st st using 3.25mm needles:
26 sts = 10cm.

MATERIALS

Jaeger pure cotton in Black: 650g.
14 claw backed studs.
1 50cm jacket zip.

BACK

Using 3mm needles, cast on 138 sts.
Row 1: K2, * p2, k2, rep from * to end.
Row 2: P2, * k2, p2, rep from * to end.
Keep rep these 2 rows to form double rib. When work measures 10cm change to 3.25mm needles and work the first and last 2 sts in st st. Work 2 more sts at either end of the row, in st st instead of rib, on each following row until only the centre 58 sts are being ribbed. Now cont in st st only. When work measures 33cm:

Shape armholes
Cast off 4 sts at beg of next 2 rows. Now dec 1 st at each end of every row until 108 sts remain. Work straight until work measures 53cm.

Shape neck
Next RS row: K37, cast off 34, k to end. Cont with this set of sts, leaving others on a holder. Dec 1 st at neck edge on next row. Work 1 row straight. Leave sts on a holder. Join yarn in at other side on neck and work to match first side. Leave sts on a spare needle.

LEFT FRONT

Using 3mm needles, cast on 50 sts and work in double rib until it measures 10cm. Change to 3.25mm needles.

Work pocket slit
Next WS row: P20, turn work, leaving other sts on a holder.
Row 2: Knit.
Cont as set until work measures 22cm. Leave these sts on a holder and return to others. Using the thumb method, cast on 20 sts to form pocket lining and then join these in at turning point and p 30. Cont working these 50 sts in st st until this section is as long as the first.
Next RS row: K30, leave the next 20 sts on a thread and work the held section of the front to end. Cont with the original 50 sts in st st. When work measures 33cm:

Shape armhole
Next RS row: Cast off 4 sts, work to end. Dec 1 st at armhole edge on every row until 36 sts remain. Now

work straight until front measures 54cm. Leave sts on a spare needle.

RIGHT FRONT

As for left front, reversing out the shapings.

BANDS

(Work 2)
Using 3mm needles, cast on 38 sts and work in double rib as on back until 54cm long. Cast off knitwise.

SLEEVES

Using 3mm needles, cast on 58 sts and work in double rib for 7cm. Change to 3.25mm needles and work the first and last 2 sts of the row in st st. Work 2 sts more in st st, instead of rib, at each end of every row, as for back, whilst inc 1 st at each end of next and every following 4th row. When only the centre 18 sts are being ribbed cont in st st only, inc as before until there are 108 sts on the needle. Now work straight until sleeve measures 44cm.

Shape sleeve head
Cast off 4 sts at beg of next 2 rows. Now dec 1 st at each end of every row until 30 sts remain. Cast off 5 sts at beg of next 4 rows and then cast off remaining 10 sts.

COLLAR

Using 3mm needles, cast on 122 sts and work in double rib for 10cm. Cast off in rib.

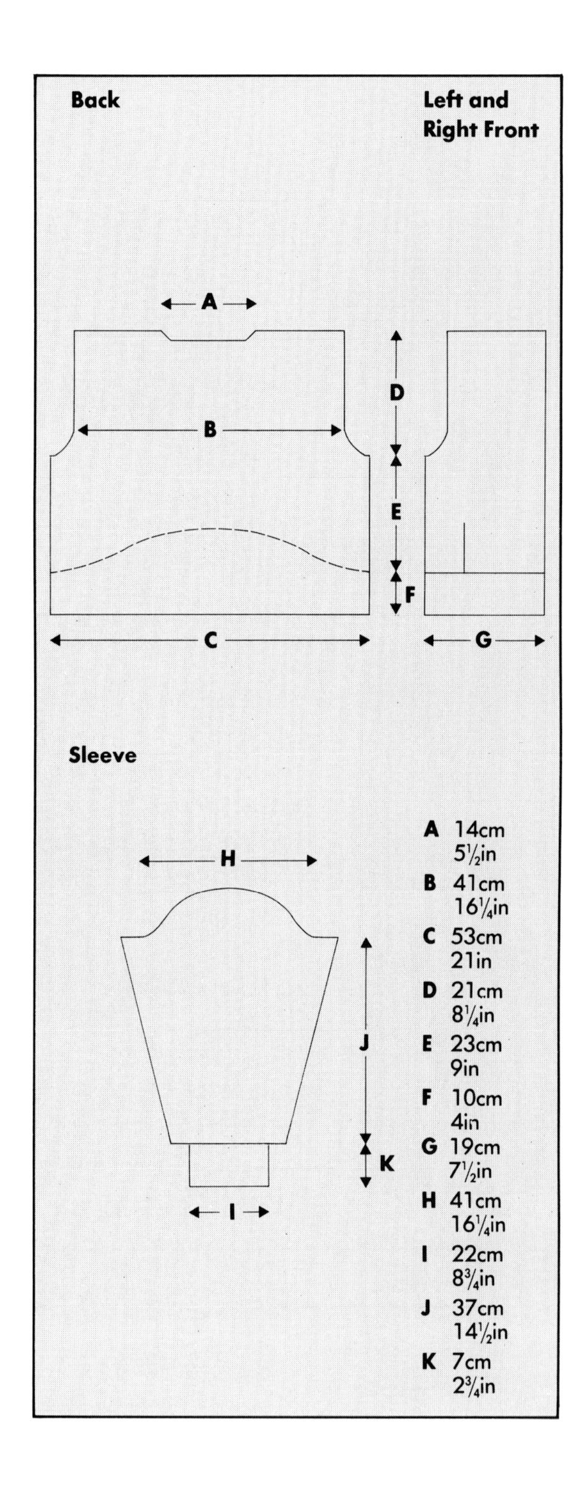

EPAULETS

(Work 2)
Using 3mm needles, cast on 8 sts.
Row 1: * K1, p1, rep from * to end.
Rep this row to form single rib for 12cm. Cast off.

POCKET BORDERS

Using 3mm needles, knit up 32 sts along the pocket slit. Work in single rib for 2.5cm. Cast off knitwise.

MAKING UP

Knit both shoulder seams tog on inside of work. Attach right band with a flat seam.

Set the zip into the band seam on the left front using a narrow backstitch. Attach the other half of the zip to the inside of the right band front edge.

Join side and sleeve seams with a flat seam. Set sleeves into armholes, pin and sew with a narrow backstitch.

Slip st the pocket lining on inside of work so that the sts do not show on RS of work. Follow the line of the ribbing up the front and then slip the sts off the thread one at a time and securing them to a row of sts as a straight guideline. Slip st down the pocket border edges.

Attach collar to form rever, as shown, stitching the cast off edge to the neckline using a flat seam.

Attach epaulets to shoulders.

Position studs as shown and bend the claws using something like a teaspoon handle.

This romantic evening top is knitted in a soft silk and wool mixture and has a lace stitch collar scattered with tiny pearls.

cultured . . . *pearl*

NEEDLES

One pair each 3.25mm and 3mm.

TENSION

Using 3.25mm needles and measured over st st: 28 sts = 10cm.

MATERIALS

Jaeger Silk and Wool, Mink: 175/200g.
Beads: 200 small round pearl beads.

BACK AND FRONT

(Worked identically)
Using 3mm needles, cast on 110/120 sts.
Row 1 (WS): * K1, p1, rep from * to end.
Row 2: * K1 tbl, p1, rep from * to end.
These 2 rows form twisted rib. Keep rep until work measures 9cm. Change to 3.25mm needles and cont in st st, inc 1 st each end of next and every following 6th row until there are 128/134 sts on the needle. Work straight until work measures 30/31cm, ending with a RS row.
Next WS row: K10/13, p to last 10/13 sts, k10/13.
Next row: Knit.
Next row: K12/15, p to last 12/15 sts, k12/15.

Shape armholes

Row 1: Cast off 8/11, purlwise, k to end.

Row 2: Cast off 8/11, knitwise, k5, p to last 6 sts, k to end.

Row 3: K6, sl 1, k1, psso, k to last 8 sts, k2 tog, k to end.

Row 4: K6, p2 tog, p to last 8 sts, p2 tog, k to end.

Rep last 2 rows and then rep row 3.

Row 8: K5, p2 tog, p to last 7 sts, p2 tog, k to end.

Shape neck

Next row: K35, cast off 30, k to end.

Cont with this set of 35 sts, leaving others on a holder.

Next row: K4, p to last 3 sts, p2 tog, p1.

Row 2: K1, sl 1, k1, psso, k to end.

Rep last 2 rows until 10 sts remain. Now work straight, cont with the 4 st garter st border at armhole edge, until work measures 17/19cm from beg of armhole shaping. Leave sts on a holder. Return to other sts, joining yarn in at neck edge and working to match first side leave sts on a spare needle.

COLLAR

Before starting, thread the beads on to the yarn, as shown.

'Bead' = bring a bead up to work (see diagram).

Using 3.25mm needles, cast on 6 sts.

Row 1 (RS): K1, (yrn, p2 tog) twice, k1.

Row 2: K1, (yrn, p2 tog) twice, k1.

Row 3: K1, (yrn, p2 tog) twice, yrn, (p1, k1) in to last st.

Row 4: K1, yrn, k2, (yrn, p2 tog) twice, k1.

Row 5: K1, (yrn, p2 tog) twice, yrn, k3, (p1, k1) in last st. Turn. K1, yrn, k2, yrn, p2 tog. Turn. Yrn, p2 tog, yrn, k3, bead, (p1, k1) in last st.

Row 6: Cast off 5. Yrn, p2 tog, k1, (yrn, p2 tog) twice, k1.

special *effect*

BEADING

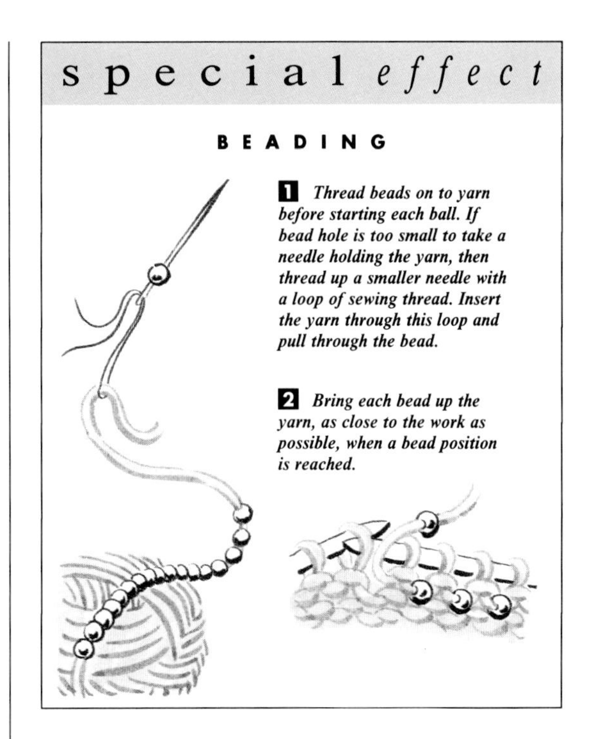

***1** Thread beads on to yarn before starting each ball. If bead hole is too small to take a needle holding the yarn, then thread up a smaller needle with a loop of sewing thread. Insert the yarn through this loop and pull through the bead.*

***2** Bring each bead up the yarn, as close to the work as possible, when a bead position is reached.*

Row 7: K1, (yrn, p2 tog) twice, (p1, k1) in next st, bead, yrn, p2 tog, yrn (p1, k1) in last st. * Turn. K3, yrn, p2 tog. Turn. Yrn, p2 tog, yrn, k2, bead, yrn, (p1, k1) in last st *.

Row 8: Cast off 5, yrn, p2 tog, yrn, k2, (yrn, p2 tog) twice, k1.

Row 9: K1, (yrn, p2 tog) twice, k2, (p1, k1) in next st, bead, yrn, p2 tog, yrn (p1 k1) in last st. Rep from * to *.

Row 10: Cast off 5, yrn, p2 tog, yrn, k4, (yrn, p2 tog) twice, k1.

Row 11: K1, (yrn, p2 tog) twice, k4, (p1, k1) in next st, bead, yrn, p2 tog, yrn, (p1, k1) in last st. Rep * to *.

Row 12: Cast off 5, yrn, p2 tog, yrn, k6, (yrn, p2 tog) twice, k1.

Row 13: K1, (yrn, p2 tog) twice, k6, (p1, k1) in next

st, bead, yrn, p2 tog, yrn, (p1, k1) in last st. Rep * to *.
Row 14: Cast off 5, yrn, p2 tog, yrn, k8, (yrn, p2 tog) twice, k1.
Row 15: K1, (yrn, p2 tog) twice, k8, (p1, k1) in next st, bead, yrn, p2 tog, yrn, (p1, k1) in last st. Rep * to *.
Row 16: Cast off 5, yrn, p2 tog, yrn, p3 tog, k7, (yrn, p2 tog) twice, k1.
Row 17: K1, (yrn, p2 tog) twice, k6, k2 tog, k1, bead, yrn, p2 tog, yrn, (p1, k1) in last st. Rep * to *.
Row 18: Cast off 5, yrn, p2 tog, yrn, p3 tog, k5, (yrn, p2 tog) twice, k1.
Row 19: K1, (yrn, p2 tog) twice, k4, k2 tog, k1, bead, yrn, p2 tog, yrn, (p1, k1) in last st. Rep * to *.
Row 20: Cast off 5, yrn, p2 tog, yrn, p3 tog, k3, (yrn, p2 tog) twice, k1.
Row 21: K1, (yrn, p2 tog) twice, k2, k2 tog, k1, bead, yrn, p2 tog, yrn, (p1, k1) in last st. Rep * to *.
Row 22: Cast off 5, yrn, p2 tog, yrn, p3 tog, k1, (yrn, p2 tog) twice, k1.
Row 23: K1, (yrn, p2 tog) twice, k2 tog, k1, bead, yrn, p2 tog, yrn, (p1, k1) in last st. Rep * to *.
Row 24: Cast off 5, yrn, (p2 tog) twice, (yrn, p2 tog) twice, k1.
Row 25: K1, (yrn, p2 tog) twice, sl 1, k2 tog, psso, k1.
Row 26: K2 tog, (yrn, p2 tog) twice, k1.
Row 27: K1, (yrn, p2 tog) twice, k1.
Row 28: K1, (yrn, p2 tog) twice, k1.
Row 29: K1, (yrn, p2 tog) twice, k1.
Row 30: K1, (yrn, p2 tog) twice, k1.
These 30 rows form the pattern.
Rep the pattern 9 times more and cast off.

p e a r l

special *effect*

BLOCKING

Carefully pin the section of work (the illustration shows a pocket flap) to required shape. Hold a steam iron a few centimetres above the knitting and allow steam to be absorbed. Leave to dry before removing pins.

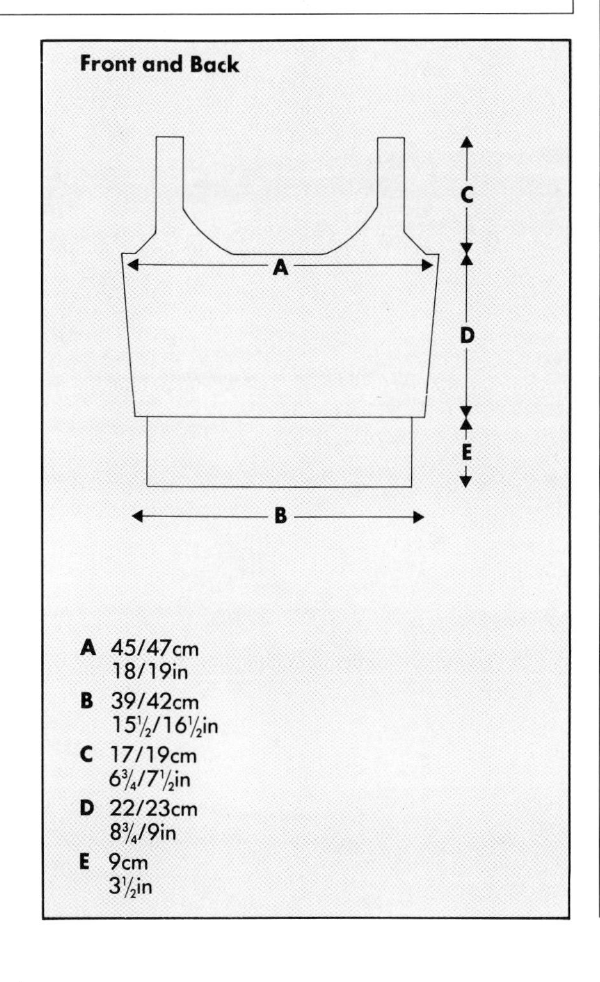

MAKING UP

Knit shoulder seams tog on inside of work. Join side seams with a flat seam over ribs and a narrow backstitch over st st.

Before attaching the collar, block into shape, pulling each point out and pinning into position (see diagram above).

Attach collar ends with a flat seam to form a circle. Place this seam at the centre of back neckline and then attach it to the neckline with a flat seam.

A creamy wool sweater in mock 'smocking' stitch with little wool nosegays embroidered at random in leaf stitch, chain stitch and french knots.

austrian ... *tyrol*

NEEDLES

One pair each 3.75mm and 4mm.

TENSION

Measured over st st, using 4mm needles:
22 sts = 10cm.

MATERIALS

Jaeger Matchmaker DK in cream: 450/500g.
DK oddments for the embroidery.

BACK

Using 3.75mm needles, cast on 90/100 sts.
Row 1: * K1, p1, rep from * to end.
Keep rep this row to form single rib for 5/7cm, inc 1 st at end of last (WS) row (91/101 sts). Change to 4mm needles and start working pattern:
Row 1 (RS): P1/6, * m1, k2, sl 1, k1, psso, p9, k2 tog, k2, m1, p1/6, rep from * to end.
Row 2: K2/7, p3, k9, p3, * k3, p3, k9, p3, rep from * to last 2/7 sts, k2/7.
Row 3: P2/7, m1, k2, sl 1, k1, psso, p7, k2 tog, k2, m1, * p3, m1, k2, sl 1, k1, psso, p7, k2 tog, k2, m1, rep from * to last 2/7 sts, p2/7.
Row 4: K3/8, p3, k7, p3, * k5, p3, k7, p3, rep from * to last 3/8 sts, k3/8.
Row 5: P3/8, m1, k2, sl 1, k1, psso, p5, k2 tog, k2, m1, * p5, m1, k2, sl 1, k1, psso, p5, k2 tog, k2, m1, rep from * to last 3/8 sts, p3/8.
Row 6: K4/9, p3, k5, p3, * k7, p3, k5, p3, rep from * to last 4/9 sts, k4/9.
Row 7: P4/9, m1, k2, sl 1, k1, psso, p3, k2 tog, k2, m1, * p7, m1, k2, sl 1, k1, psso, p3, k2 tog, k2, m1, rep from * to last 4/9 sts, p4/9.
Row 8: K5/10, p3, k3, p3, * k9, p3, k3, p3, rep from * to last 5/10 sts, k5/10.
Row 9: P5/10, m1, k2, sl 1, k1, psso, p1, k2 tog, k2, m1, * p9, m1, k2, sl 1, k1, psso, p1, k2 tog, k2, m1, rep from * to last 5/10 sts, p5/10.

Row 10: K6/11, p3, k1, p3, * k11, p3, k1, p3, rep from * to last 6/11 sts, k6/11.
Row 11: P6/11, put yarn to back of work and placing the RH needle between the 2 sts which are **now** the 7th and 8th on the LH needle, pull a loop through to the front, put it on LH needle and knit it tog with the first st on this needle (called 'draw tog'), k2, p1, k3, * p11, draw tog, k2, p1, k3 rep from * to last 6/11 sts, p6/11.
Row 12: K6/11, p3, k1, p3, * k11, p3, k1, p3, rep from * to last 6/11 sts, k6/11.
Row 13: P5/10, k2 tog, k2, m1, p1, m1, k2, sl 1, k1, psso, * p9, k2 tog, k2, m1, p1, m1, k2, sl 1, k1, psso, rep from * to last 5/10 sts, p5/10.
Row 14: K5/10, p3, k3, p3, * k9, p3, k3, p3, rep from * to last 5/10 sts, k5/10.
Row 15: P4/9, k2 tog, k2, m1, p3, m1, k2, sl 1, k1, psso, * p7, k2 tog, k2, m1, p3, m1, k2, sl 1, k1, psso, rep from * to last 4/9 sts, p4/9.
Row 16: K4/9, p3, k5, p3, * k7, p3, k5, p3, rep from * to last 4/9 sts, k4/9.
Row 17: P3/8, k2 tog, k2, m1, p5, m1, k2, sl 1, k1 psso, * p5, k2 tog, k2, m1, p5, m1, k2, sl 1, k1, psso, rep from * to last 3/8 sts, p3/8.
Row 18: K3/8, p3, k7, p3, * k5, p3, k7, p3, rep from * to last 3/8 sts, k3/8.
Row 19: P2/7, k2 tog, k2, m1, p7, m1, k2, sl 1, k1, psso, * p3, k2 tog, k2, m1, p7, m1, k2, sl 1, k1, psso, rep from * to last 2/7 sts, p2/7.
Row 20: K2/7, p3, k9, p3, * k3, k9, p3, rep from * to last 2/7 sts, k2/7.
Row 21: P1/6, * k2 tog, k2, m1, p9, m1, k2, sl 1, k1, psso, p1/6, rep from * to end.
Row 22: K1/6, * p3, k11, p3, k1/6, rep from * to end.
Row 23: P1/6, k3, p11, * draw tog, k2, p1, k3, p11, rep from * to last 4/9 sts, k3, p1/6.
Row 24: As row 22.
These 24 rows form the pattern. Cont in pattern unless otherwise instructed. Inc 1 st each end of next and every following 5th row until there are 113/123 sts on the needle, keeping new sts in reverse st st. Work 10 rows straight.

Shape armholes
Cast off 4 sts at beg of next 2 rows. Now dec 1 st each end of every row until 91/101 sts remain. Work straight until 6 patterns have been completed from the beg. Leave sts on a spare needle.

FRONT

As for back, until 5 patterns have been worked.

Shape neck
Row 1 of next patt: Pattern 37/42 sts, cast off 17 sts, patt to end.
Cont with this set of sts, leaving others on a holder. Dec 1 st at neck edge on every row until 30/33 sts remain. Now dec 1 st at neck edge on every alt row until 27/30 sts remain. Work straight until 6 patterns have been worked from beg. Leave sts on a holder. Return to other side of neck, join yarn in at neck edge and shape to match first side. Leave sts on a spare needle.

SLEEVES

Using 3.75mm needles, cast on 54 sts and work in single rib for 7/8cm, inc 1 st on last (WS) row, (55 sts). Change to 4mm needles and cont in pattern as for back, inc 1 st each end of next and every following 6th/4th row, keeping new sts in reverse st st, until there are 91 sts. Work straight until row 22 of the 5th pattern repeat has been worked.

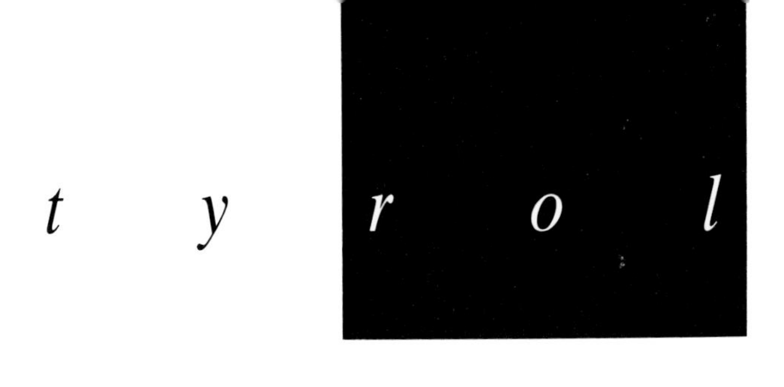

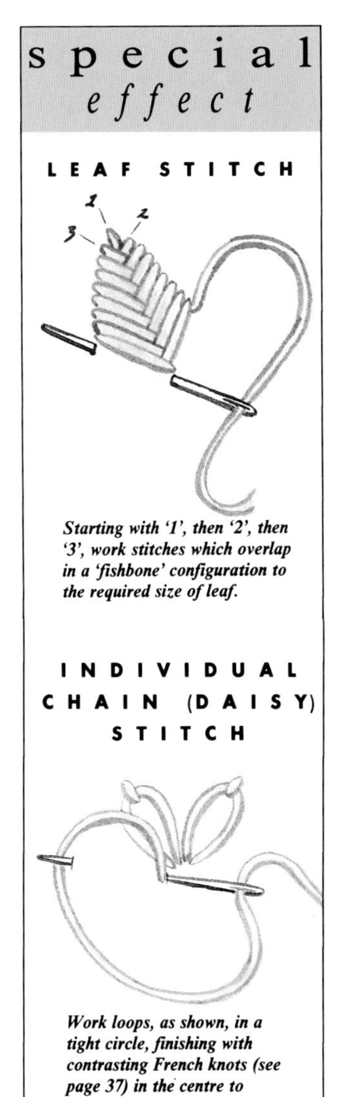

Starting with '1', then '2', then '3', work stitches which overlap in a 'fishbone' configuration to the required size of leaf.

Work loops, as shown, in a tight circle, finishing with contrasting French knots (see page 37) in the centre to represent the stamens.

Shape sleeve head

Cast off 4 sts at beg of next 2 rows. Now dec 1 st at each end of every row until 73 sts remain. Now dec 1 st each end of every alt row until 59 sts remain. Now dec 1 st each end of every row again until 29 sts remain. Cast off 8 sts at beg of next 2 rows. Cast off remaining 13 sts.

NECKBAND

First knit right shoulder seam tog on the inside of the work.

Using 3.75mm needles and with RS facing, knit up 24 sts down the left front, 17 across centre, 24 up other side and then knit across the 37/41 back neck sts (102/106 sts). Purl the first row and then work in single rib for 5cm, ending with a RS row. Now knit 2 rows and then cast off knitwise using a larger needle to keep the cast off-edge loose.

MAKING UP

Knit the second shoulder seam tog and join the neckband edges with a flat seam. Join side and sleeve seams with a flat seam.

Set sleeves in, distributing any fullness to the top of the shoulder. Attach with a narrow backstitch.

Embroider random flower motifs, as shown, using leaf stitch and individual chain (daisy) stitch (see diagram left) and French knots (see diagram page 37).

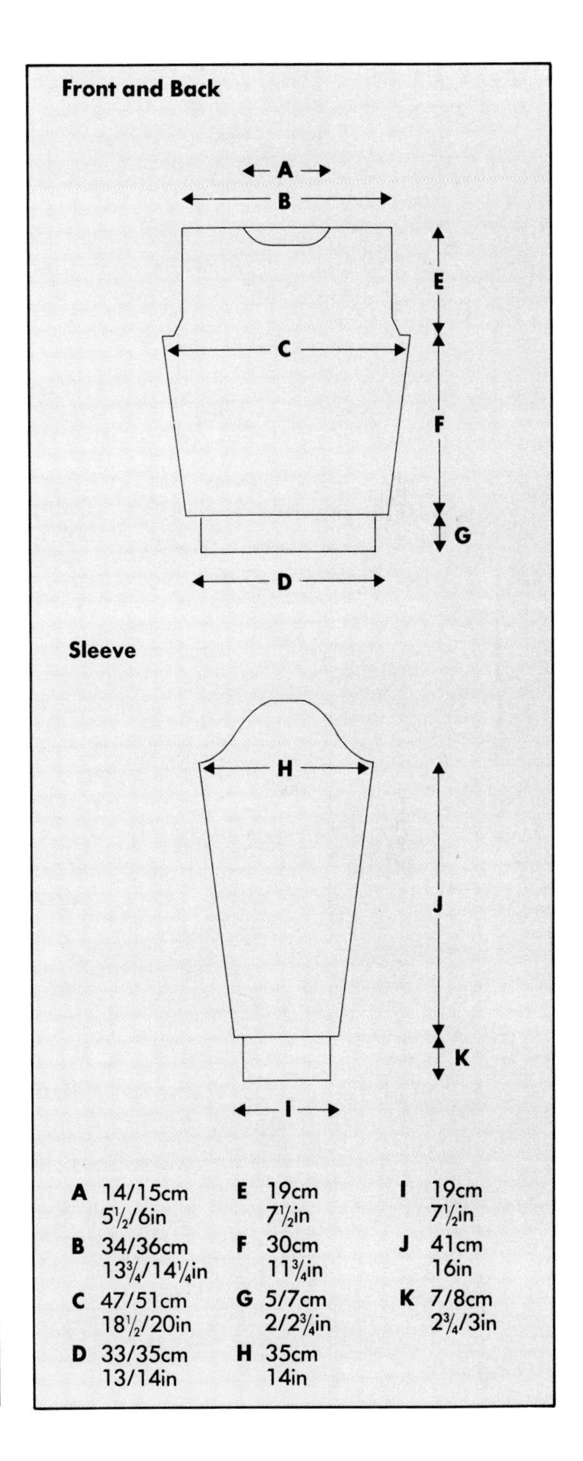

A dramatic trompe l'oeuil sweater decorated with eye-catching costume jewellery which is knitted and then embroidered in gold.

costume . . . *jewel*

NEEDLES

One pair each 4mm and 3.75mm needles and one medium cable needle.

TENSION

Measured over st st, using 4mm needles:
24 sts = 10cm.

MATERIALS

Jaeger Matchmaker DK in Black: 450/450/500g.
Jaeger Gaugin in Beauly Green, Cairn Blue, Inca and Venetian: one ball each colour.
Twilleys Double Gold: 50g.

FRONT

Using 3.75mm needles and base colour, cast on 106/110/114 sts.
Row 1 (WS): * K1, p1, rep from * to end.
Row 2: * K1-b, p1, rep from * to end.
Keep rep these 2 rows to form single twisted rib for 12cm. Change to 4mm needles and cont in st st, inc 3 sts evenly across first row (109/113/117 sts). When work measures 26/27/28cm, begin working from graph, starting with a RS row and working armhole and neck shaping as shown, leaving centre neck sts on a holder rather than casting off.

BACK

As for front but omitting the colour design and neck shaping. Leave back neck sts on a holder.

SLEEVES

Using 3.75mm needles and base colour, cast on 46/48/50 sts and work in single twisted rib for 6cm. Change to 4mm needles and cont in st st, inc 1 st each end of next and every following 7th/7th/7th row until there are 78/82/84 sts on the needle. Now work straight, until sleeve measures 45/47/49cm.

Shape sleeve head

Cast off 2 sts at beg of next 2 rows. Now dec 1 st each end of every row until 54/60/60 sts remain. Now dec 1 st each end of every alt row until 32/34/34 sts remain. Cast off 6 sts at beg of next 4 rows. Cast off remaining 8/10/10 sts.

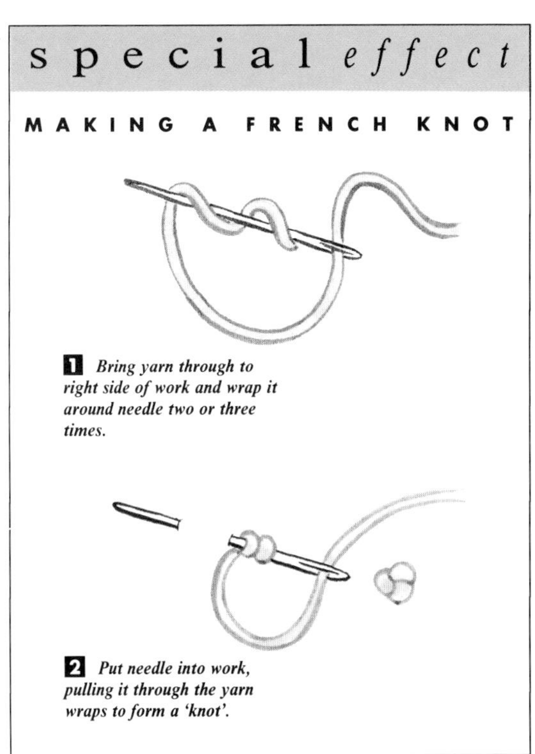

special *effect*

MAKING A FRENCH KNOT

1 *Bring yarn through to right side of work and wrap it around needle two or three times.*

2 *Put needle into work, pulling it through the yarn wraps to form a 'knot'.*

c o s t u m e

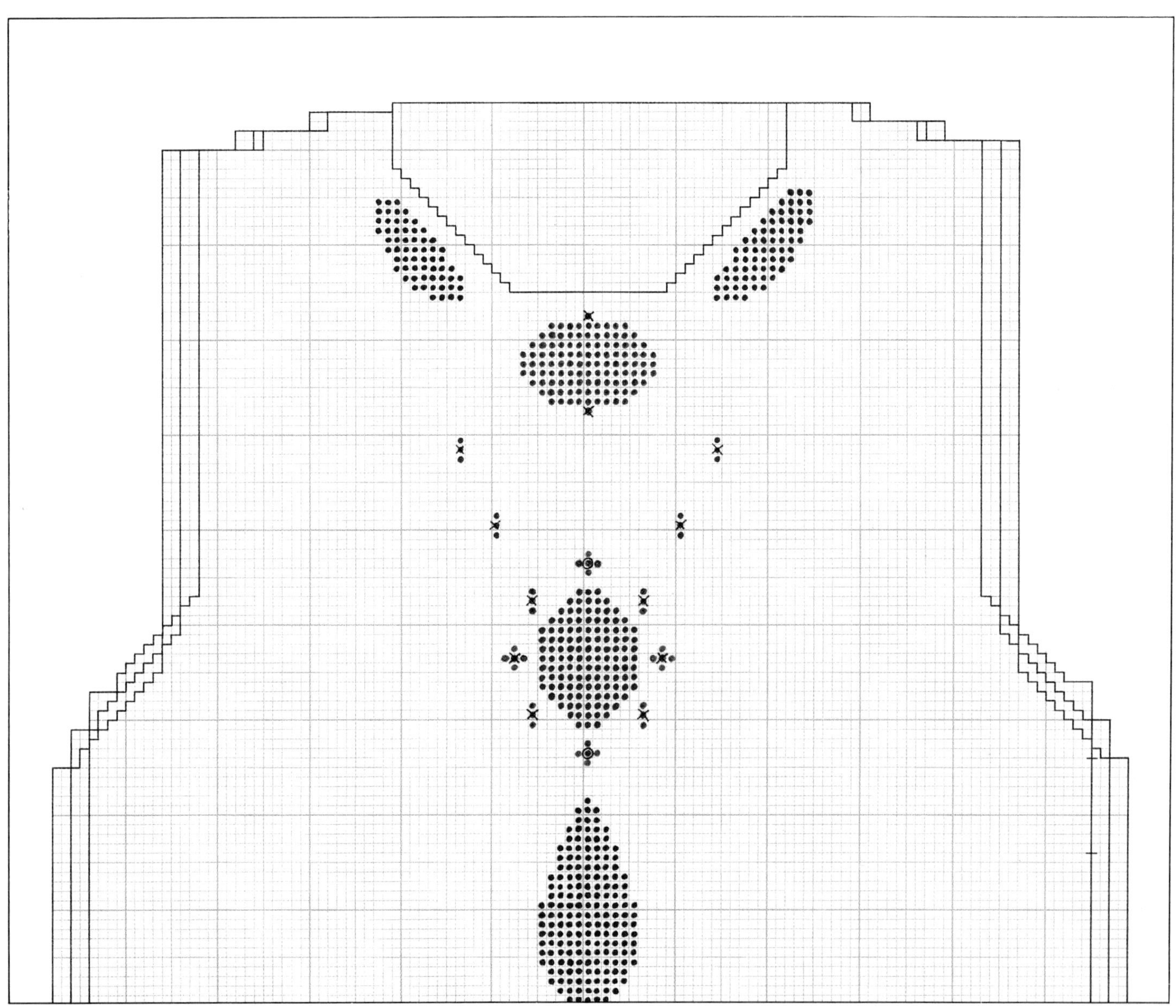

o = make 5 sts out of 1st, turn
K5, turn
P3, turn
K3, turn
lift 2nd, 3rd, 4th, 5th sts over 1st

x = make 3 sts instead of 5

j e w e l

TURTLE NECK

Join the right shoulder seam with a narrow back-stitch. Using 3.75mm needles, base colour and with RS facing, knit up 22/24/26 sts down left side of front, knit across the 17 held sts, knit up 22/24/26 sts up other side of front, knit across the 43 back neck sts (104/108/112 sts). Purl the first (WS), row and then work in single twisted rib for 5cm. Cast off in rib.

GOLD CHAIN

Using gold and 4mm needles, cast on 6 sts.
Row 1 (RS): K2, p2, k2.
Row 2: P2, k2, p2.
Row 3: As row 1.
Row 4: P2, k2 tog, yarn around needle twice, p2.
Row 5: K2, p 'yarn around needle' as a single stitch, p1, k2.
Row 6: P2, k2, p2.
Row 7 + 8: As rows 1 + 2.
Row 9: Slip the first 4 sts on to a CN at front of work, k2, sl 2 purl sts from CN back to LH needle and then put the cable needle with remaining 2 sts to back of work, in-between the two main needles, purl the 2 sts on LH needle and then k those on CN.
Row 10: P2, k2, p2.
These 10 rows form the pattern. Keep rep until the 'chain' is long enough to go around the neck, as shown in close up.

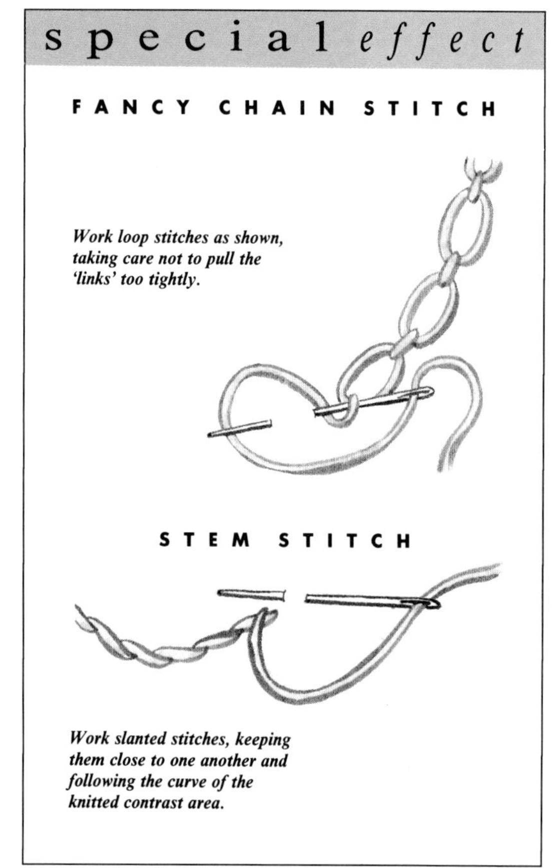

MAKING UP

Join right shoulder seam tog with a backstitch and join the edges of the neckband with a flat seam.

Work French knots as positioned on graph (see diagram page 37 and graph page 38). Using gold, outline the 'gems' in stem stitch and join the jewels with cable chain stitch (see diagrams above).

Join the ends of the cable 'chain' with a flat seam and then position around neck and stitch down.

Now join side and sleeve seams with a flat seam. Set the sleeves into armholes and sew with a narrow backstitch.

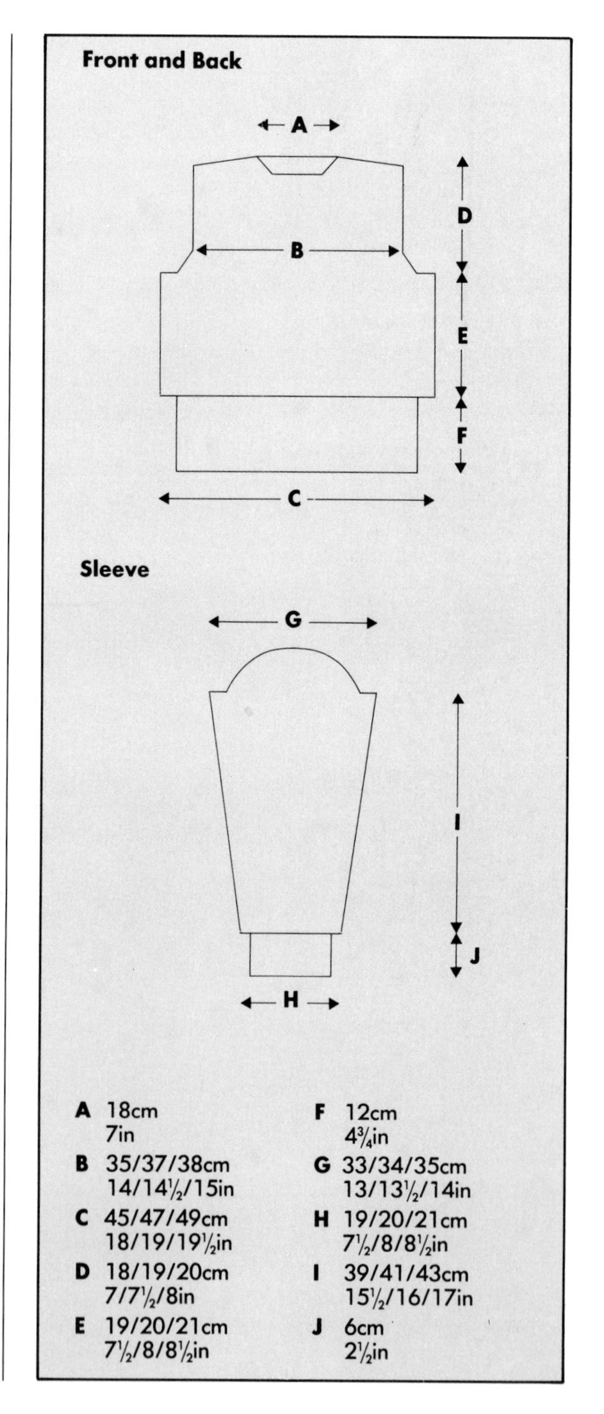

A very feminine, figure-hugging sweater, with a glamorous scooped neckline decorated with three-dimensional knitted roses and leaves.

rambling ... *rose*

NEEDLES

One pair each 3mm, 3.25mm and 3.75mm.

TENSION

Using 3.75mm needles and measured over st st:
24 sts = 10cm.

MATERIALS

Jaeger pure cotton in 'Linen': 450/500g,
'Silk Peach': 50g.

BACK AND FRONT

(Worked identically)
Using 3.25mm needles, cast on 114/120 sts.
Row 1 (WS): * K1, p1, rep from * to end.
Row 2: * K1 tbl, p1, rep from * to end.
These 2 rows form single twisted rib. Rep until work measures 3cm. Change to 3.75mm needles and st st,

r a m b l i n g

dec 1 st each end of next and every following 6th row until you have 92/98 sts. Change to 3.25mm needles and cont in st st, dec as before until there are 90/96 sts on the needle. Work 12 rows straight, change back to 3.75mm needles and cont in st st, inc 1 st each end of next and every following 4th/5th row until there are 110/116 sts. Work straight until work measures 44/46cm from beg, ending with a RS row.

Shape raglans and neck

Row 1: Cast off 1/3 sts, p to end.

Row 2: Cast off 1/3 sts, k 37/38, turn work leaving remaining sts on a holder.

Next row: P2, p2 tog, p to last 4 sts, p2 tog, p2.

Row 2: K to last 4 sts, sl 1, k1, psso, k2.

Keep rep last 2 rows until 11 decs have been worked at neck edge. Now cont by dec 1 st each end of every alt row at both edges until 2 sts remain. Work 2 tog and fasten off remaining st. Return to held sts, leave centre 32 sts on the holder and work other side of neck to match first.

SLEEVES

Using 3.25mm needles cast on 50/54 sts. Work in single twisted rib for 7cm. Change to 3.75mm needles and cont in st st, inc into every 11th st across the first row (54/58 sts). Now inc 1 st each end of next and every following 7th row until you have 80/84 sts. Work straight until work measures 42/44cm, ending with a WS row.

Shape raglans

Cast off 1/3 sts at beg of next 2 rows. Now dec 1 st each end of next and every alt row, as for body, until 44 sts remain. Leave sts on a holder.

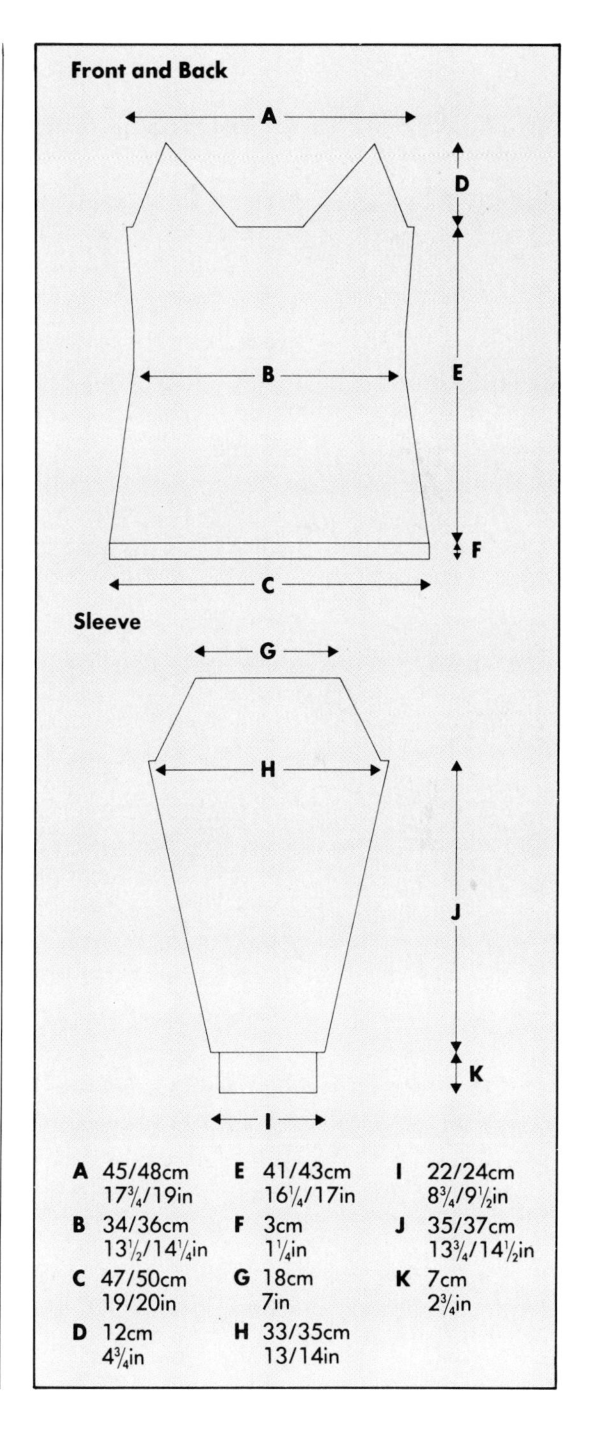

NECKBAND

First join all raglans, except the left sleeve back, using a flat seam.

Using 3.25mm needles and with RS facing, knit across the 44 sts from top of left sleeve, knit up 26 sts down left side, 32 sts across front, 26 sts up other side and then the same again around other sleeve and back (256 sts). Purl the first row and then cont in twisted single rib until band is 4cm deep. Change to 3mm needles and cont until band is 8cm deep. Cast off in rib.

LEAVES

(Work four in each colour)
Using 3.25mm needles, cast on 3 sts using thumb method.
Row 1: Purl.
Row 2: Inc, k1, inc.
Row 3: K2, p1, k2.
Row 4: K1, inc, k1, inc, k1.
Row 5: K3, p1, k to end.
Row 6: K1, inc, k3, inc, k1.
Row 7: K4, p1, k to end.
Row 8: K1, inc, k5, inc, k1 (11 sts).
Now work straight in garter st, keeping the centre st in st st, for 8 rows.
Row 17: K2 tog, k3, p1, k3, k2 tog.
Row 18: K2 tog, k to last 2 sts, k2 tog.
Cont as set, dec 1 st each end of every row, keeping centre st in st st until 3 sts remain.
Next row: Sl 1, k2 tog, psso. Fasten off.

LARGE ROSE

(Work two in each colour)
Using 3.25mm needles cast on 2 sts and purl them.
Row 2: K1, inc.
Row 3 and all odd rows: Purl.
Row 4: K1, inc, k1.
Row 6: K2, inc, k1.
Row 8: K3, inc, k1 (6 sts).
Cont in st st, dec 1st on every row at shaped edge until 2 sts remain. Now increase at the shaped edge, as before, until there are 8 sts. Decrease back to 2 sts and then increase again until there are 10 sts. Decrease back to 2 sts and then purl 2 tog and fasten off.

SMALL ROSES

(Work one in each colour)
As for large roses but work the first 2 'petals' only and then fasten off.

MAKING UP

Join raglan and neckband seam. Join side and sleeve seams with a flat seam.

Coil each rose around itself with the smallest 'petal' inside and the smooth side of the st st on the outside. Stitch through the petals at the base of each rose.

Place petals and roses around neckline and attach firmly, taking stitches straight through to the WS of work, so that they will stay in position.

A long-line fitted waistcoat in silky cotton, decorated with ornamental swirls of knitted braids and twisted cords and finished with gold buttons.

oriental ... *gold*

NEEDLES

One pair each 3.25, 3.75mm, 4mm and 7mm.

TENSION

Measured over st st, using 3.75mm needles:
24 sts = 10cm.

MATERIALS

Jaeger Pure Cotton: 450/500g of 'Paprika'.
1 ball Jaeger Gaugin 'Inca'.
1 ball Twilleys Doublegold in Gold.
8 buttons for fastening.
Assorted gems/buttons/beads as required.

BACK

Using 3.25mm needles, cast on 124/134 sts and knit 10 rows. Change to 3.75mm needles and cont in st st but knitting the first and last 5 sts on every row for a

further 15 rows. Now cont in st st only, dec 1 st at each end of next and every following 9th/8th row. When 110/118 sts remain start working darts.
Next RS row: K35, sl 1, k1, psso, k36/44, k2 tog, k to end.
Work a dart row thus on every 4th row, working the

decs so that they line up, immediately above the previous ones, whilst cont to shape sides as before. When 88/92 sts remain work straight for 5/10 rows. Now inc 1 st at each end of next and every following 8th row. Meanwhile work inc darts (by working into the st on the row below the next st and then the st itself), on next and every following 4th row, to line up with the previous dec darts. When 5 sets of inc darts have been worked, cont to inc at the sides only until you have 112/116 sts on the needle. Work straight until back measures 54/56cm from beg, ending with a RS row.

Next row: K6, p to last 6 sts, k6.
Row 2: Knit.
Row 3: K8, p to last 8 sts, k8.
Row 4: Knit.

Shape armholes

Next row: cast off 5 knitwise, k5, p to last 10 sts, k10.
Row 2: Cast off 5 purlwise, k to end.
Row 3: K5, p2 tog, p to last 7 sts, p2 tog, k5.
Row 4: K5, sl 1, k1, psso, k to last 7 sts, k2 tog, k to end.

Rep these last 2 rows until 84/88 sts remain. Now work straight, maintaining the 5 st garter st border at either end of the row until the work measures 75/77cm.

Shape shoulders

Next 2 rows: Work to last 10 sts, turn work and repeat.
Rows 3 + 4: Work to last 19/20 sts, turn work and repeat.
Rows 5 + 6: Work to last 28/30 sts, turn work and repeat.
Leave sts on a spare needle.

LEFT FRONT

Using 3.25mm needles, cast on 67/72 sts. Knit 10 rows.

Next (WS) row: K5, put these on a pin, p to last 5 sts, k to end.

Change to 3.75mm needles and cont with the 62/67 sts, working in st st with a 5 st garter st border at side edge for 15 rows in all. Now cont in st st only, dec 1 st at side edge on every following 9th/8th row until 55/59 sts remain.

Work dart

Next RS row: K30, sl 1, k1, psso, k to end.

Work a dart thus on every 4th row, lining them up one above another, whilst cont to dec at side edge. When 44/46 sts remain work 5/10 rows straight. Now inc 1 st at side edge on next and every following 8th row whilst working an inc dart (as on back), lined up with previous dart. When 5 incs have been made for the dart, cont inc, at side edge only, until there are 56/58 sts. Now work straight until work measures 52/54cm from beg.

Shape neck

Dec 1 st at neck edge on next and every following 5th row. Meanwhile when work measures 54/56cm:

Work armband and shape armhole

As for back, working 9 decs after casting off 5 sts. Now work this edge straight whilst cont to dec at neck edge until 28/30 sts remain. Work straight until work measures 20cm from start of armhole shaping.

Shape shoulder

Next WS row: P to last 10 sts, turn and k to end.
Rows 3 + 4: P to last 19/20 sts, turn and k to end.
Leave sts on a holder.

special *effect*

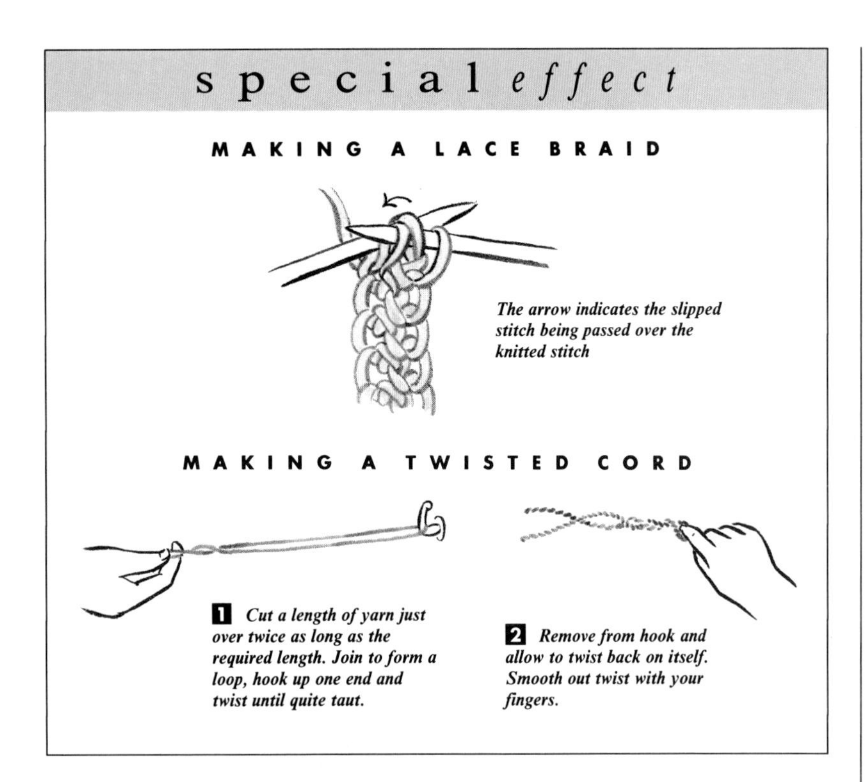

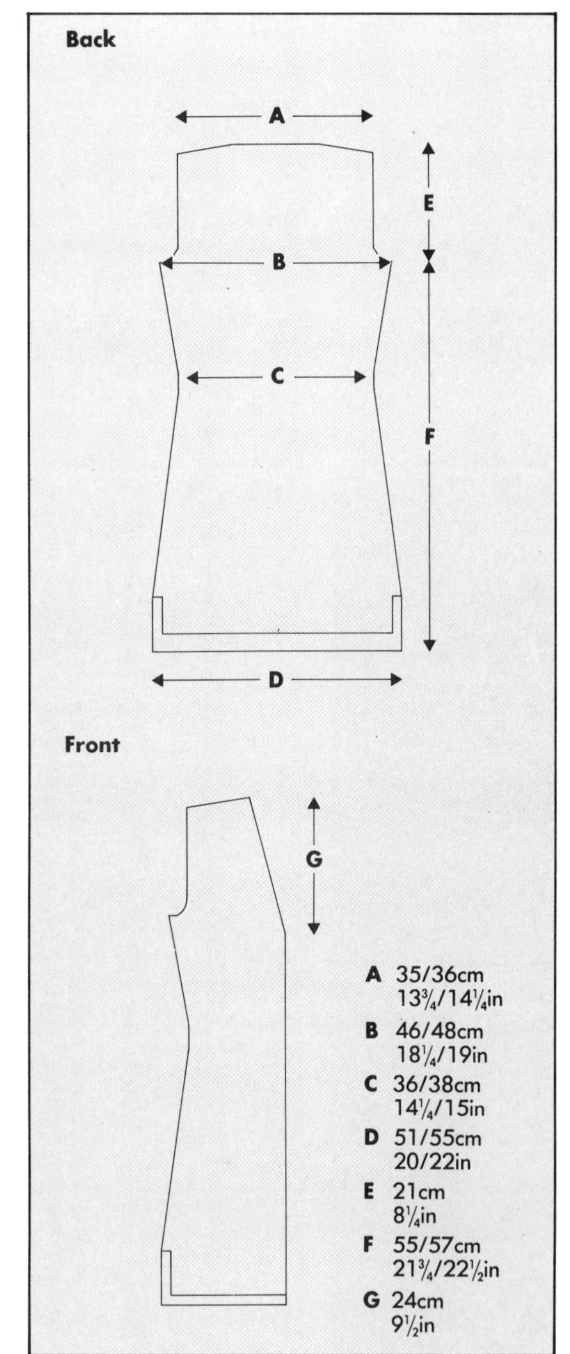

RIGHT FRONT

As for left front, reversing out the shapings.

LEFT BAND AND COLLAR

Slip the 5 held sts onto 3.25mm needles and cont in garter st until the band is long enough to reach the start of the neck shaping.

Shape collar

Inc 1 st on the inside edge, i.e. that nearest the neck edge, on the next and every following 12th row until you have 12 sts. Work straight until it is long enough to reach the centre back neck. Leave on a holder.

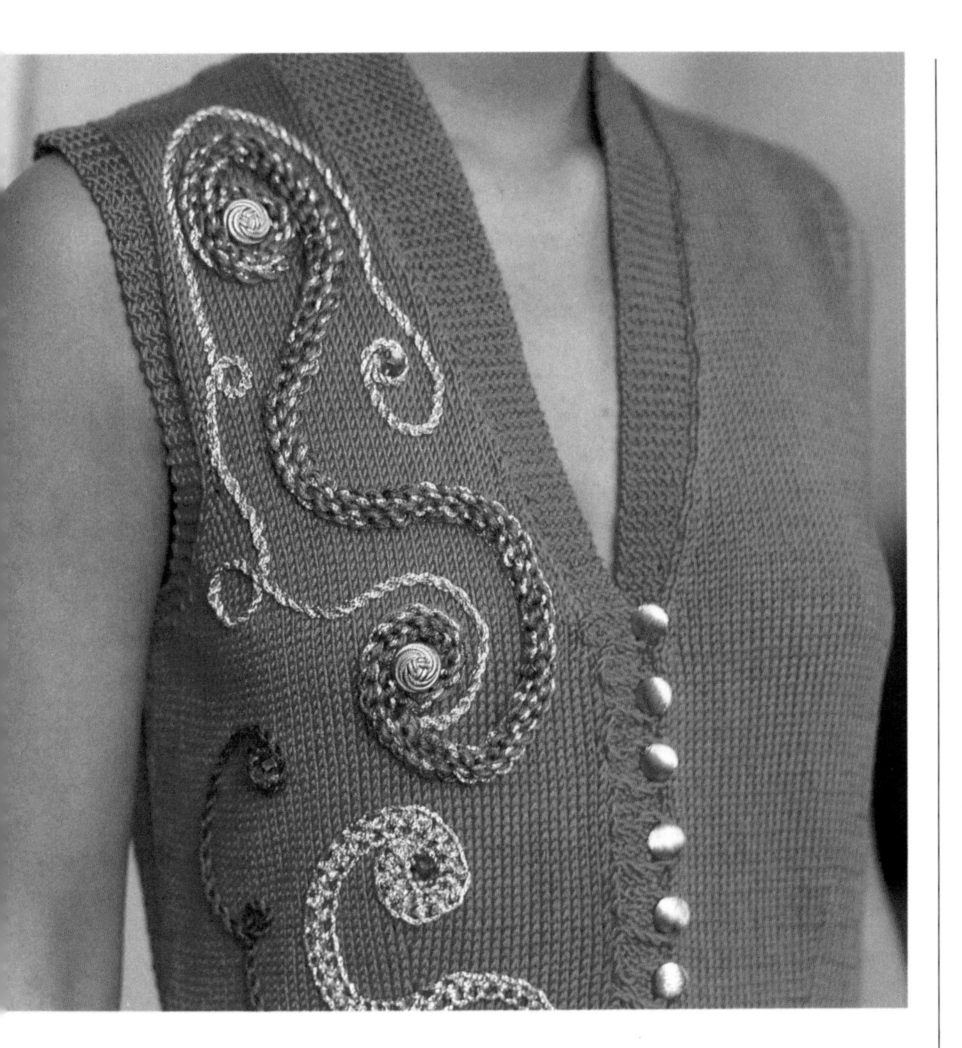

RIGHT BAND AND COLLAR

Exactly as for left – there are no buttonholes.

LACE BRAID

(See diagram opposite.) Using Doublegold and 4mm needles, cast on 2 sts. The braid is formed by repeating the following row every row for required length (approx 60cm used for the sample):
Yo needle to back, sl 1 p-wise, k1, psso.
NB Take care not to confuse the strand of the 'yo' with the 'sl 1, k1, psso'.

KNITTED BRAID

Using 1 end of each colour and 7mm needles, cast on 88 sts and then cast them off fairly loosely. Pull cord out to its full length.

TWISTED CORDS

(See diagram opposite.)
Work 1 in each colour to a finished length of approx 80cm.

MAKING UP

Knit one shoulder seam tog, cast off the 28 back neck sts, knit 2nd shoulder seam tog. Knit collar pieces tog to form a seam at centre back neck. Carefully pin bands and collar into position, distributing the fabric evenly. Attach with a flat seam.

Attach the fastening buttons, evenly spaced, with the top one at the point where the neck shaping starts and with button one 20cm below. Arrange the self-coloured cord to form button loops to accommodate the buttons with a swirl at either end. Arrange the other braids and cords into swirls. Pin and then slip stitch into place. Position the gems/buttons/beads to hide the ends of each braid (as shown in close up). Join the side seams with a flat seam, leaving the vents with the garter st border open.

A classic roll-neck sweater with a simple 'patchwork' texture stitch, knitted in one colour and then Swiss darned with tapestry motifs.

medieval *tapestry*

NEEDLES

One pair each 4mm and 3.75mm.

TENSION

Measured over st st, using 4mm needles:
24 sts = 10cm.

MATERIALS

Rowan Designer DK, colour no 639: 800g.
DK oddments for Swiss darning.

BACK

Using 3.75mm needles, cast on 156 sts.
Row 1: * K1, p1, rep from * to end.
Keep rep this row to form single rib for 6cm, ending with a RS row. Purl the next row, inc 3 sts evenly across it (159 sts). Change to 4mm needles and work pattern from graph. The graph repeats 6 times across the row and then the first 3 sts of the graph are worked to complete the row. When work measures 47cm:

Shape armholes
Cast off 10 sts at beg of next 2 rows (139 sts). Work straight, cont to keep in pattern until 6 patts have been worked in depth. Leave sts on a spare needle.

FRONT

As for back until 5 repeats have been worked in depth.

Shape neck
Next (RS) row: Pattern 60 sts, cast off 19 sts, patt to end. Cont with this set of sts, leaving others on a holder. Dec 1 st at neck edge on every row until 48 sts

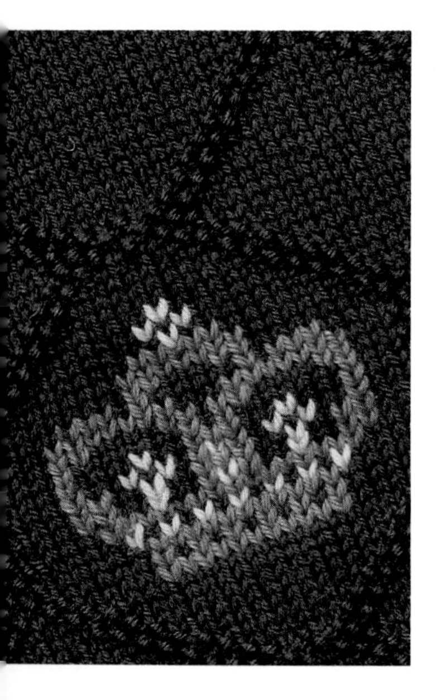

• = knit st on WS row
Purl st on RS row

remain (keeping in patt throughout). Work straight until front matches back. Leave sts on a holder. Return to other sets of sts, join yarn in at neck edge and work to match first side. Leave sts on a spare needle.

SLEEVES

Using 3.75mm needles, cast on 50 sts and work in single rib for 6cm, ending with a RS row. Purl the next row, inc into every 10th st, (55 sts). Change to 4mm needles and work in patt (2 reps across row plus the first 3 sts of graph at end of row). Inc 1 st each end of next and every following 4th row, working new sts into patt as you go, until there are 107 sts. Work straight until 3.5 repeats in depth have been worked. Cast off loosely.

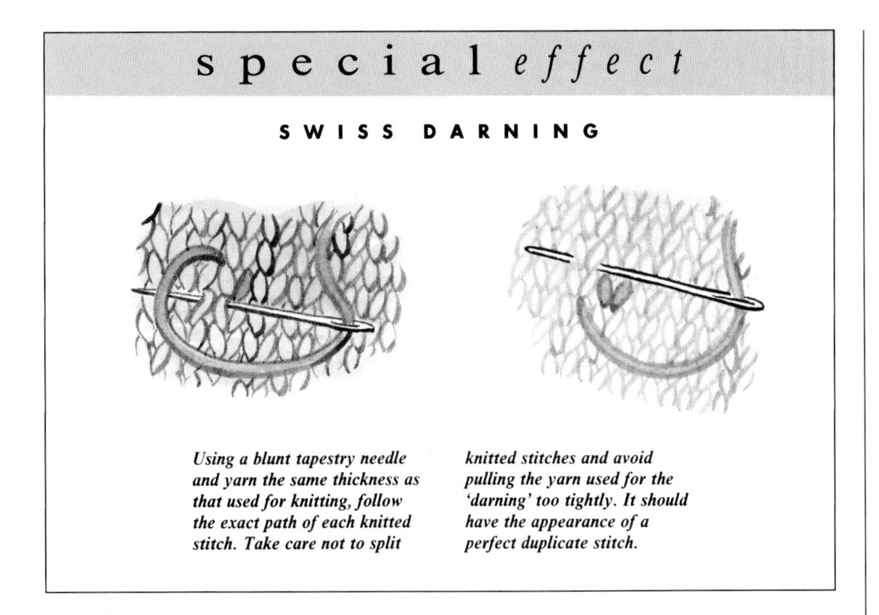

special *effect*

SWISS DARNING

Using a blunt tapestry needle and yarn the same thickness as that used for knitting, follow the exact path of each knitted stitch. Take care not to split knitted stitches and avoid pulling the yarn used for the 'darning' too tightly. It should have the appearance of a perfect duplicate stitch.

ROLL NECK

First knit the right shoulder seam tog on inside of work. Using 3.75mm needles and with RS facing, knit up 27 sts down left side of neck, 19 across front, 27 up other side and then knit across 43 back neck sts, leaving other shoulder sts on holder (116 sts). Purl the first row and then work in single rib for 12cm. Cast off in rib.

MAKING UP

Knit left shoulder seam tog and join neck edges with a flat seam. Open out body and attach sleeves so that the right angle of the sleeve top fits into that created by the cast off edges. Attach with a flat seam. Now join the sleeves and side seams with a flat seam.

Swiss darn the motifs from the graphs, as illustrated above.

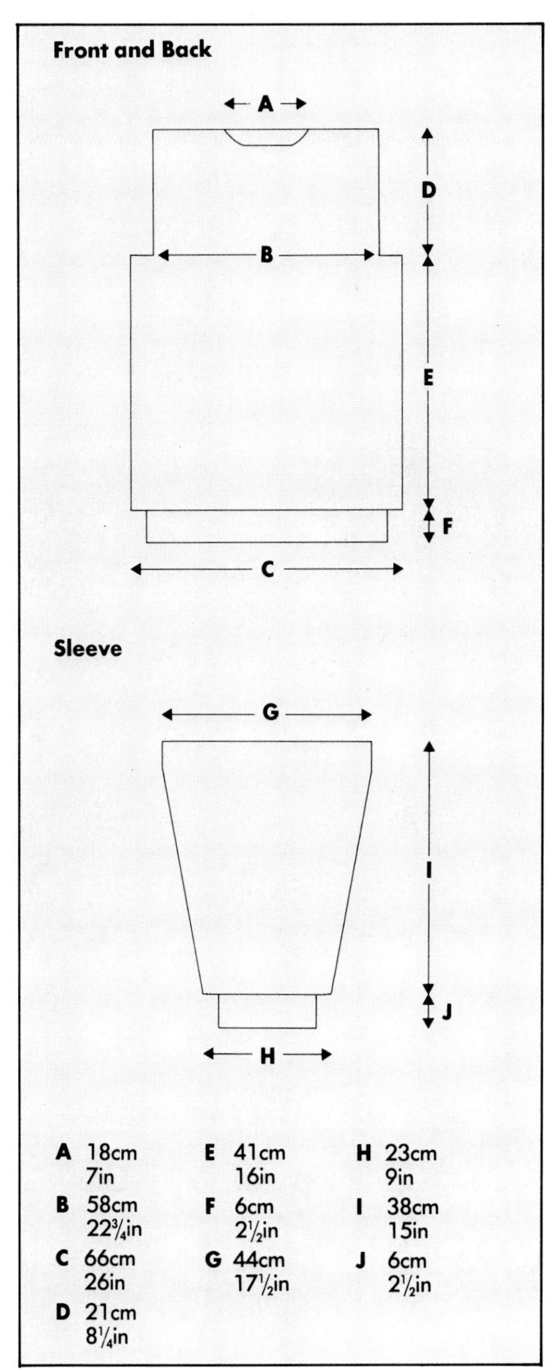

A pure-silk waistcoat based on a design from the eighteenth century and featuring a delicate embroidered rosebud motif in bullion stitch and backstitch.

georgian . . rosebud

NEEDLES

One pair each 3mm and 3.25mm.

TENSION

Measured over st st, using 3.25mm needles:
28 sts = 10cm.

MATERIALS

Rowan Mulberry Silk – Gunmetal: 90/100g.
Natural: 130/140g.
1 skein each – pink and green embroidery silk.
8 buttons.
One metre of Gunmetal 3cm ribbon.

BACK

Using Gunmetal and 3mm needles, cast on 118/130 sts.

Row 1 (WS): * K1, p1, rep from * to end.
Row 2: * K1 tbl, p1, rep from * to end.
These 2 rows form single twisted rib. When work measures 3cm change to 3.25mm needles and cont in st st, inc 1 st each end of first row (120/132 sts). When work measures 23/24cm:

Shape armholes

Cast off 7 sts at beg of next 2 rows. Now dec 1 st each end of every row until 76/88 sts remain. Work straight until work measures 24/25cm from start of armhole shaping, ending with a RS row.

Shape neck and shoulders

Next row: P17/23, cast off 42, p9, turn work and k9. Leave these 17/23 sts on a holder and join yarn in at neck edge of other side of neck.
Next row: K9/12, turn work and p9/12. Leave sts on a holder.

LEFT FRONT

Using natural and 3.25mm needles, cast on 3 sts and purl them.
Next row: K1, M1, k to end.
Row 2: P1, M1, p to last st, M1, p1.
Keep rep last 2 rows until there are 58 sts on the needle. (2nd size only: Work front edge straight but cast on 3 sts at beg of next 2 RS rows.) Now work both sides straight for 20/21cm, ending with a WS row.

Shape armhole
Cast off 7 sts at beg of next row and then dec 1 st at this edge on every row until 36/42 sts remain. Now work this edge straight but immediately:

Shape neck
Dec 1 st at neck edge on next and every following 3rd row until 17/23 sts remain. Work straight until work measures 24/25cm from start of armhole shaping, ending with a RS row.

Shape shoulder
Next row: P9/12, turn and k9/12. Leave sts on a holder.

RIGHT FRONT

As for left front, reversing out shapings so that you knit the first row after casting on.

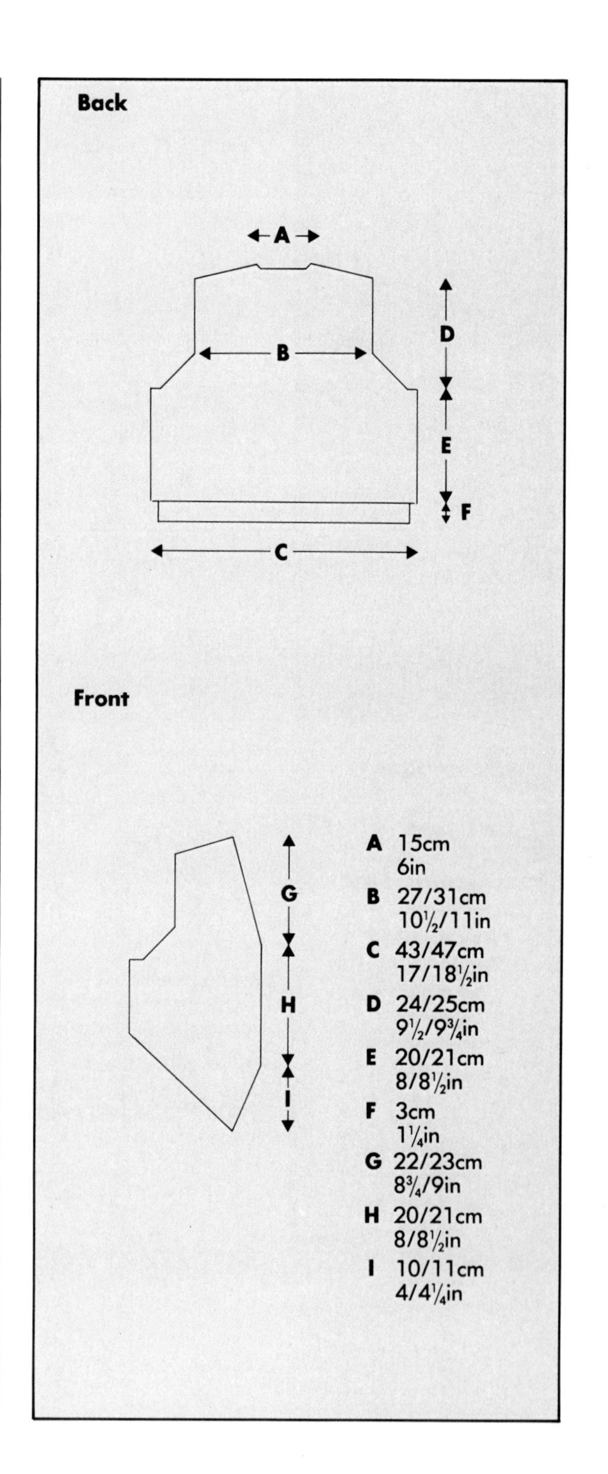

BUTTONBAND

(First knit both shoulder seams tog on inside of work.)
When fitting the band around the work it should be very slightly stretched and pinned into position for accuracy.
Using 3mm needles and natural, cast on 9 sts and work in single twisted rib until it is long enough to reach from the side seam to the bottom point of front.

Shape mitre
Next (WS) row: Rib 6, turn work.
Row 2: Rib to end.
Rows 3 + 4: Rib 4, turn and rib to end.
Rows 5 + 6: Rib 2, turn and rib to end.
Now work straight until it is long enough to reach the point where the front shaping stops.

Shape mitre
Next (WS) row: Rib 4, turn work.
Row 2: Rib to end.
Now work straight until the band reaches the centre back neck. Cast off. Mark 8 button positions equally from top to bottom of straight front edge.

BUTTONHOLEBAND

Work as for buttonband, reversing the angles of the mitres and working buttonholes to correspond with button markers thus:
Buttonhole on a RS row: Rib 3, yo, work 2 tog, rib to end.
Next row: Rib, working the yo as a stitch.

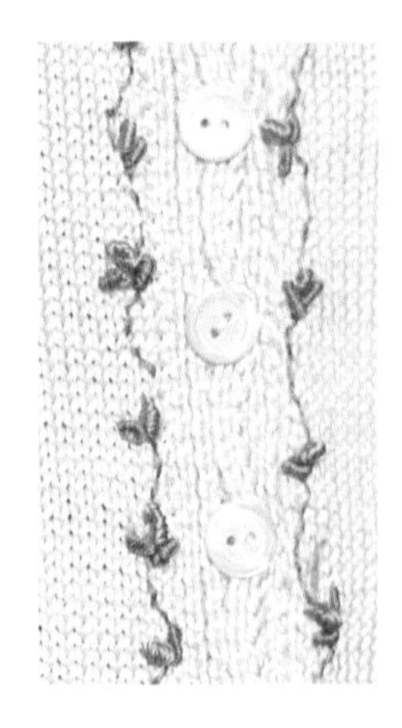

special *effect*

BLOCKING

Carefully pin pocket flap to the required shape, pulling a point down from the cast-on edge. Hold a steam iron a few centimetres above knitting and allow steam to be absorbed. Leave to dry before removing pins.

BULLION STITCH

Place needle in and out of work and then wrap the thread around needle several times before putting needle back into work.

LEFT ARMBAND

Using natural, 3mm needles and with RS facing, knit up 126/132 sts from front to back. Purl the first row and then work in single twisted rib for 2.5cm. Cast off in rib.

RIGHT ARMBAND

As for left, but knit up from back to front.

POCKET FLAPS

(Work 2)
Using 3.25mm needles, cast on 30 sts and work in st st for 4cm, ending with a WS row. Cast off knitwise.

MAKING UP

Join the cast off ends of the bands tog with a flat seam and centre this at the back neck. Carefully pin bands into position, taking great care to distribute them evenly, and attach with a flat seam. Join side seams similarly.

Block fake pocket flaps, pulling the lower (cast on) edge down in the centre to form a slight curve (see diagram). Position on fronts, as in photograph, and slip stitch down.

Attach buttons. Attach ribbon ties to back, as shown.

Embroider roses and leaves using bullion stitch (see diagram left) and the stalk using backstitch.

A sleeveless top and edge-to-edge jacket worked in a lace pattern using silk/wool and trimmed with faceted beads. The neck and armholes are edged with crochet.

lace *and . . crystal*

NEEDLES

One pair 3.75mm and small crochet hook. (One pair 3.75mm needles also needed for the top.)

TENSION

Using 3.75mm needles, cast on 25 sts and work in lace pattern, omitting 'clusters' which fall at edge of work. Work 28 rows and cast off loosely. This piece should measure 9cm from row edge to row edge, measured at the widest part.

MATERIALS

	Jacket	Top
Jaeger Silk/wool in Brick red:	350g	125g
Small glass/plastic beads:	2000	500

ABBREVIATIONS

A cluster = with yarn at back, slip the specified no of sts from left to right needle, bring yarn to front, slip sts back to left needle, put yarn to back, slip sts to

right needle and then cont working normally.

NB Always omit clusters if they fall at the edge of the work, purl the sts instead.

B1 = pull a bead up as close to the work as it will go, slip the next st and work the following st normally, leaving the bead sitting on the strand in front of the slipped st.

(See page 60 for threading beads.)

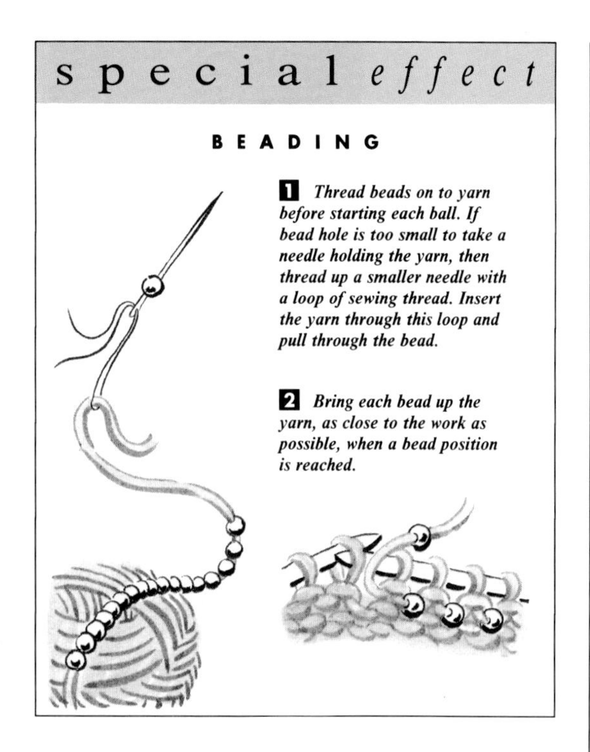

JACKET BACK

Before starting a new ball of yarn, thread up about 200 beads. Using 3.75mm needles, cast on 157 sts using the thumb method to give this edge elasticity. Work lace pattern, as follows:

Row 1: (RS) K2, * yo, (k1 tbl, p1, B1, p1) 5 times, k1 tbl, yo, k1, rep from *, ending k2.

Row 2: P4, * (k3, p1) 4 times, k3, p5, rep from * ending p4.

Row 3: K2, * yo, k1 tbl, yo, (k1 tbl, p3) 5 times, (k1 tbl, yo) twice, k1, rep from * ending k2.

Row 4: P6, * (k3, p1) 4 times, k3, p9, rep from * ending p6.

Row 5: K2, * yo, k1 tbl, yo, sl 1, k1, psso, yo, (k1 tbl, p2 tog, p1) 5 times, k1 tbl, yo, k2 tog, yo, k1 tbl, yo, k1, rep from * ending k2.

Row 6: P8, * (k2, p1) 4 times, k2, p13, rep from * ending p8.

Row 7: K2, * k1 tbl, (yo, sl 1, k1, psso) twice, yo, (k1 tbl, p2) 5 times, k1 tbl, yo, (k2 tog, yo) twice, k1 tbl, k1, rep from * ending k2.

Row 8: P9, * (k2, p1) 4 times, k2, p15, rep from * ending p9.

Row 9: K3, * (yo, k2 tog) twice, yo, k1 tbl, yo, (k1 tbl, p2 tog) 5 times, (k1 tbl, yo) twice, (sl 1, k1, psso, yo) twice, k3, rep from * to end.

Row 10: P11, * (k1, p1) 4 times, k1, p 19, rep from * ending p11.

Row 11: K1, sl 1, k1, psso, * (yo, k2 tog) 3 times, k1 tbl, yo, (k1 tbl, p1) 5 times, k1 tbl, yo, k1 tbl, (sl 1, k1, psso, yo) 3 times, sl2, k1, p2sso, rep from * ending last rep k2 tog, k1.

Row 12: As row 10.

Row 13: K1, * (k2 tog, yo) twice, k2 tog, k1, k1 tbl, yo, (sl 1, k1, psso) twice, sl 1, k2 tog, psso, (k2 tog) twice, yo, k1 tbl, k1, sl 1, k1, psso, (yo, sl 1, k1, psso) twice, k1, rep from * ending k3.

Row 14: P3, * p7, cluster 5, p7, cluster 3, rep from * ending p3 instead of cluster 3.

These 14 rows form the pattern. Rep pattern 18 times in all. Cast off loosely.

JACKET RIGHT FRONT

Using 3.75 needles, cast on 91 sts and work in patt as for back until 17 patts have been worked.

Shape neck

Cast off 24 sts at beg of first row of next patt, patt to

c r y s t a l

end (67 sts). Now cont straight until the 18th patt is complete. Cast off loosely.

JACKET LEFT FRONT

As for right front but when it comes to the neck shaping, cast off the last 23 sts on the row and then join yarn in again at the neck edge to cont working as for other side, working 2 tog at neck edge on final row (67 sts). Cast off loosely.

SLEEVES

Using 3.75mm needles, cast on 69 sts and work in patt as for back, inc 1 st each end of every 8th row, working new sts in st st, until there are 101 sts on the needle. Cont straight until 11 patts are complete. Cast off loosely.

MAKING UP

Sew shoulder seams with a narrow backstitch, easing slightly more in from the fronts than the back so that the back neck opening measures 12cm across when the seams are finished.

Open out body and pin sleeves into position whilst flat. Let them find their own depth. Do not bunch them into an imaginary armhole. Attach with a narrow backstitch and only then join side and sleeve seams similarly.

Crochet a 'shell' edging around the neck thus: Work 4 tr into first cast off st of right side of neck. Now miss a stitch, work a d.c. into next st, miss another st and then rep from beg. Work right around neckline, missing out more than one knitted edge st

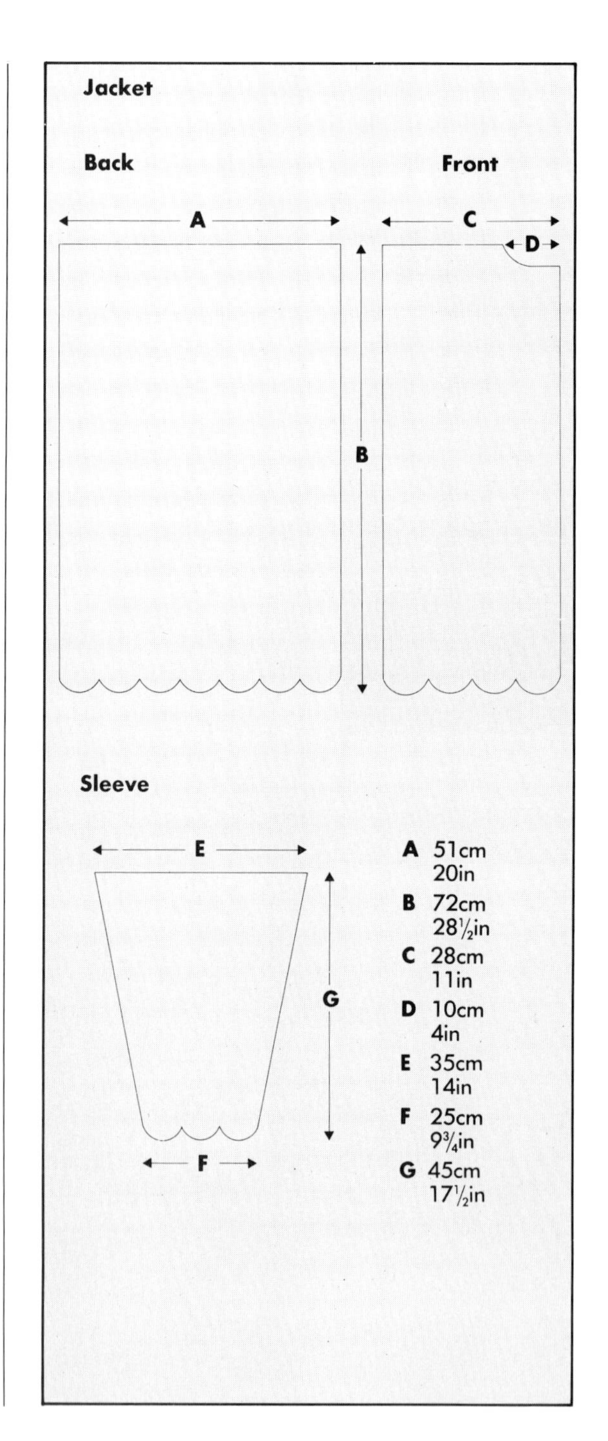

where necessary, ending on 4 tr at left side. Block out front edging, especially at neck so that the edge is not too 'frilly'. (See diagram on page 72.)

TOP BACK

Using 3.75mm needles and threading approx 120 beads on to yarn before starting, cast on 135 sts and work in patt as for jacket back until 8 reps in depth have been worked. Change to 3.25mm needles.
Next row: * P3, k1 tbl rep from * to last 3 sts, p3.
Row 2: K3, * p1, k3, rep from * to end.
Rep these last 2 rows twice.
Row 7: * P1, B1, p1, k1 tbl, rep from * to last 3 sts, p1, B1, p1.
Row 8: As row 2.
These 8 rows form the yoke patt.

Shape armholes

Next row: Cast off 8 sts, patt to end.
Row 2: Cast off 8 sts, patt to end.
Now dec 1 st each end of every row until 97 sts remain. Now work straight, in patt, until work measures 51cm. Leave sts on a spare needle.

TOP FRONT

As for back until yoke measures 11cm.

Shape neck

Next row: Patt 37 sts, cast off 23 sts, patt to end. Cont with this set of sts leaving others on a holder. Dec 1 st at neck edge on every row until 30 sts remain. Now dec 1 st at this edge on every alt row until 26 sts remain. Now work straight until front matches back.

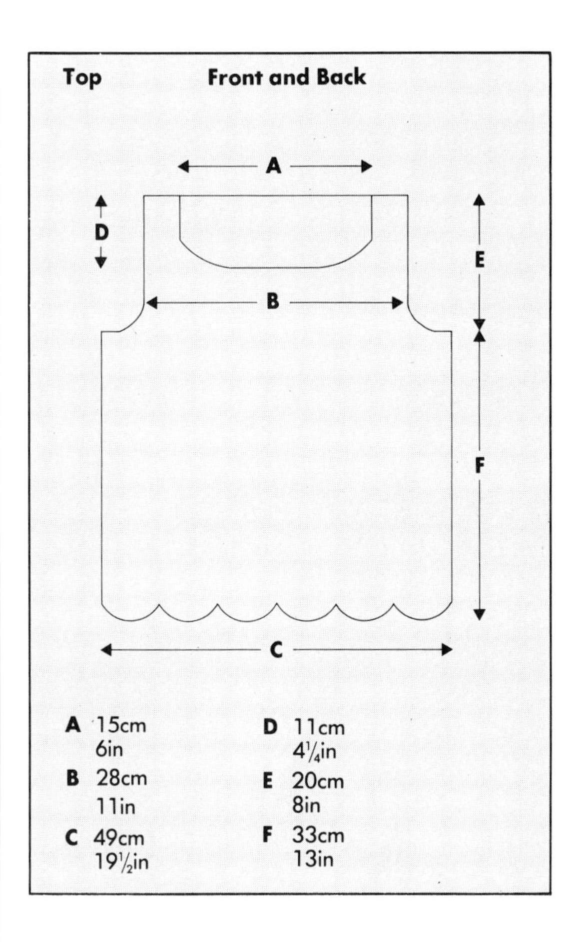

Leave sts on a holder. Join yarn in at other side of neck and work to match first. Leave sts on the needle.

MAKING UP

Knit first shoulder seam tog on inside of work, cast off 45 back neck sts, knit 2nd shoulder seam tog.

Join side seams with a narrow backstitch.

Crochet a 'shell' edge around neck and armholes, as for jacket neck but ending on a dc.

This midnight blue sweater is created in velvety chenille and decorated with moon and star jewels. Any beads or gems may of course be used.

midnight . . . *sky*

NEEDLES

One pair each 4mm and 3.75mm.

TENSION

Measured over st st, using 4mm needles:
18 sts = 10cm.

MATERIALS

Jaeger Chenille in blue: 600g.
Stones: 2 'moons' and approx 60 stars and 10 tiny stones.

BACK AND FRONT

(Worked identically)
Using 3.75mm needles, cast on 104 sts.
Row 1: K1, p1, rep from * to end.
Keep rep this row to form single rib. When rib measures 7cm, change to 4mm needles and cont in st st, inc 3 sts evenly across first row (107 sts). When work measures 49cm:

Shape armholes

Cast off 8 sts at beg of next 2 rows (91 sts).
Now work straight until work measures 58cm.

Shape neck

Next RS row: K45, turn work leaving remaining sts on a holder.
Row 2: Cast off 2 sts purlwise, p to end.
Row 3: K to last 2 sts, k 2 tog.
Rep last 2 rows until 21 sts remain. Now work straight until work measures 72cm. Leave sts on a holder. Return to other side of neck, leave centre st on a pin and then shape this side to match first, reversing out shapings. Leave sts on a holder.

m i d n i g h t

SLEEVES

Using 3.75mm needles, cast on 40 sts and work in single rib for 13cm. Change to st st, inc into every 4th st across the first row (50 sts). Now change to 4mm needles and cont in st st, inc 1 st each end of every 5th row until there are 82 sts. Work straight until sleeve measures 45cm. Cast off loosely.

NECKBAND

First knit the right shoulder seam tog on inside of work. Using 3.75mm needles and with RS facing, knit up 20 sts down the straight part of left side, put a marker on the needle, knit up 30 sts down the slope, put another marker on needle, knit the centre st off the pin, knit up 30 sts up slope, put another marker on the needle, knit up 20 sts up the right side and then exactly the same around back neck (202 sts).

NB The st after each marker is an 'axial' st and is kept in st st throughout.

Work in single rib, working 2 sts tog at either side of each of the 6 axial sts until neckband is 2cm deep. Cast off in rib, working decs on this row as on previous ones.

MAKING UP

Knit left shoulder seam tog on inside of work and join neckband seam with a flat seam. Open out body and fit sleeve top into armhole. Pin and attach with a flat seam. Only now join sleeve and side seams with a flat seam.

Lay the garment flat with something like a magazine inside to separate the layers. Arrange stones in a fairly 'free-hand' manner and attach with ordinary

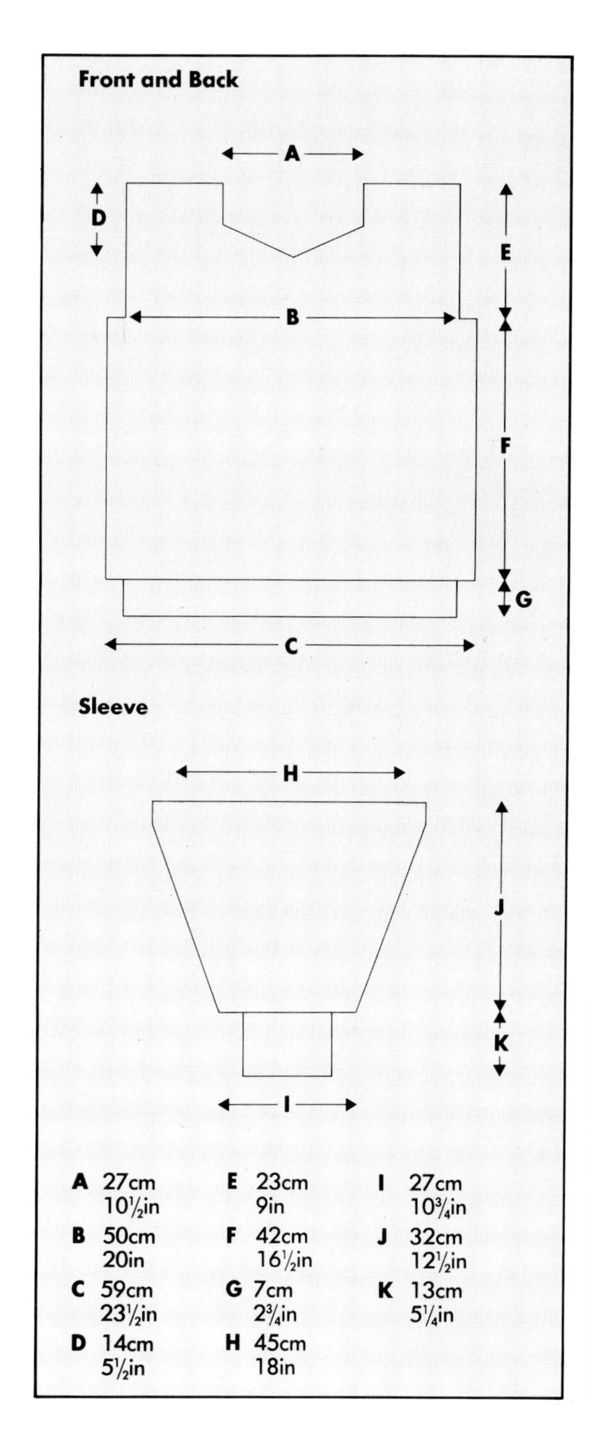

sewing thread, keeping the garment flat and working from bottom, up. **NB** Instead of fastening off the thread after each stone, loosely run the thread up the back of the sts to the next stone position, secure it there and then attach stone.

A cowboy-style heavy-weight jacket which is perfect for the great outdoors. It has generous pockets and is trimmed with knitted fringes.

country ... and western

NEEDLES

One pair each 5mm and 4.5mm.

TENSION

Measured over st st using 5mm needles:
17 sts = 10cm.

MATERIALS

Rowan 'Magpie' aran wool, in colour 503 (Comanche): 1100g.
9 plastic button bases for covering with yarn.
One pair of large straight-edged shoulder pads.

BACK

Using 4.5mm needles, cast on 104 sts.
Row 1: * K1, p1, rep from * to end.
Row 2: * P1, k1, rep from * to end.
These 2 rows form moss st, rep once. Change to 5mm needles and cont in st st until work measures 52cm.

Shape armholes
Cast off 4 sts at beg of next 2 rows. Now dec 1 st each end of every row until 80 sts remain. Work straight until it measures 74cm from beg. Leave sts on a spare needle.

LEFT FRONT

Using 4.5mm needles, cast on 56 sts. Work in moss st for 4 rows. Change to 5mm needles.
Next (RS) row: K50, turn work leaving last 6 sts on a pin.
Cont in st st. When work measures 49cm:

Shape neck
Next WS row: P2, p2 tog, p to end.
Cont to dec, as set, on every 4th row. Meanwhile when work measures 52cm:

c o u n t r y

Shape armhole

Next RS row: Cast off 4 sts, k to end.

Dec 1 st at this edge on every row for 8 rows (meanwhile cont to shape neck as before). Now work armhole edge straight and cont to dec at neck edge until 27 sts remain. Work straight until front matches back. Leave sts on a holder.

RIGHT FRONT

As for left, reversing out shapings.

LEFT BAND AND REVER

Slip sts off pin on to a 4.5mm needle. Work in moss st until the band is long enough to reach the point where the neck shaping starts, when very slightly stretched.

Next RS row: Inc 1, moss to end.

Cont in moss st, inc 1 st at this edge on every 4th row until you have 18 sts. Work 2 rows straight. Cast off, in pattern.

Mark 9 button positions with the first at the point where the band sts were taken from the pin, the last 1cm down from the start of the neck shaping and the rest equally spaced between.

RIGHT BAND AND REVER

As for left, reversing out shapings and working buttonholes to correspond with button markers, thus:

Buttonhole row (RS): Moss 2, cast off 1, moss to end.

Next row: Moss, casting on 1 st immediately above that cast off on previous row.

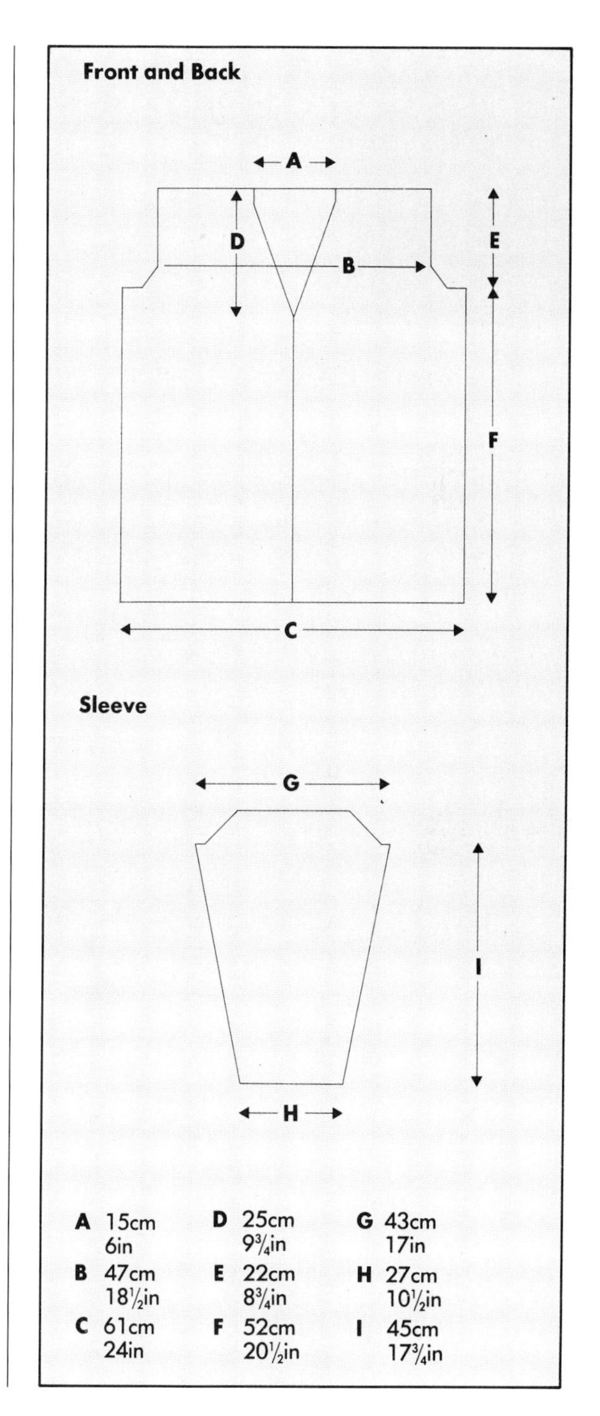

SLEEVES

Using 4.5mm needles, cast on 46 sts and work in moss st for 4 rows. Change to 5mm needles and cont in st st, inc 1 st each end of next and every following 7th row until there are 74 sts. Work straight until sleeve measures 45cm.

Shape sleeve head
Cast off 4 sts at beg of next 2 rows. Now dec 1 st each end of every row until 18 sts remain. Cast these off loosely.

COLLAR

Using 4.5mm needles, cast on 16 sts and work in moss st for 38cm. Cast off in pattern.

BACK FRINGE

** Using 4.5mm needles, cast on 3 sts and knit them.
Row 1: Purl 3 and then without turning work, cast on 14 sts using the thumb method. Now turn work.
Row 2: Cast off 14 sts knitwise (to form actual fringe), k2 and without turning work, cast on 2 sts by the thumb method, turn work.
Row 3: Cast off 2 purlwise, p2 and then without turning work, cast on 14 sts, turn.
Row 4: As row 2.
Rep these last 2 rows until 4 fringes have been worked in all. Now work 4 fringes 16 sts in length, then the same number with 18 sts, 20 sts, 22 sts and 24 sts. **
Now work 2 fringes which are 26 sts (26 fringes in all).
Now work the mirror image, ending with 4 fringes of 14 sts each.
Final row: Cast off 2, p2, turn work.
Cast off 3 sts.

special *effect*

BLOCKING

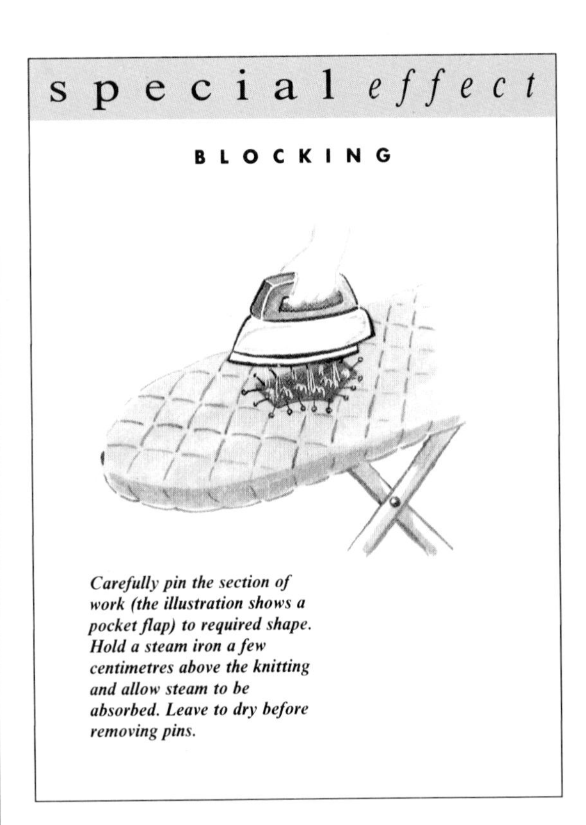

Carefully pin the section of work (the illustration shows a pocket flap) to required shape. Hold a steam iron a few centimetres above the knitting and allow steam to be absorbed. Leave to dry before removing pins.

FRONT FRINGE

Right: Work from ** to ** and then work the final row and cast off.
Left: As for right but starting with the 24 st fringes and finishing with the 14 st ones.

SLEEVE FRINGE

Right: Work from ** to ** but instead of working 4 fringes of each length, work 6 (36 in all). Work final row and cast off.
Left: As for right but starting with long fringes and finishing with short.

POCKETS

(Work 2)
Using 4.5mm needles, cast on 32 sts.
Row 1: K2, p30.
Row 2: K30, p2 and without turning work cast on 12 sts, turn.
Row 3: Cast off 12, k1, p to end.
Cont as set, working 6 fringes of 12 sts, 8 fringes of 16 sts and then 6 of 12 sts again (20 fringes in all).
Final row: K30, p2.
Cast off purlwise.

MAKING UP

Knit one shoulder seam tog on inside of work, cast off 26 back neck sts, knit second shoulder seam tog.

Block out the fringe pieces so that each individual strand is pulled out straight and the measurement is the same as the garment piece for which it is meant (see diagram opposite).

Attach fringes to the fronts, back and sleeves while the garment is still in pieces, using a running stitch through the centre line of a stitch so that it will not show on the RS of work. Fold the fringe back over the pockets and attach these squarely to the fronts using a slip st.

Attach bands and revers to fronts using a flat seam. Attach collar similarly, as shown. Join side and sleeve seams with a flat seam and set sleeves in similarly.

Wrap yarn around button bases as illustrated on packet and attach buttons to bands. Add shoulder pads.

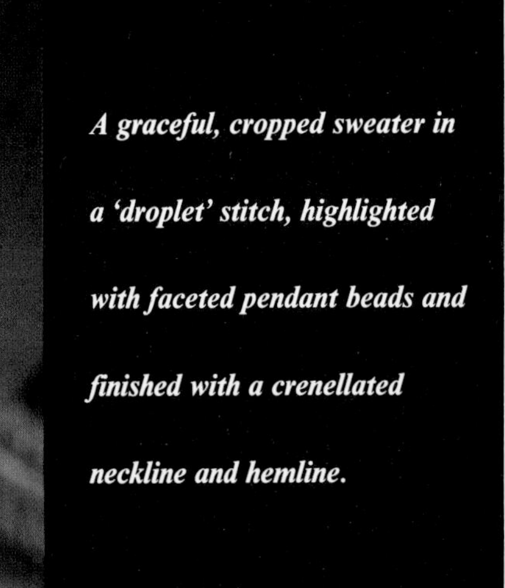

A graceful, cropped sweater in a 'droplet' stitch, highlighted with faceted pendant beads and finished with a crenellated neckline and hemline.

r a i n . . *d r o p s*

NEEDLES

One pair of 3.25mm needles, one medium-sized cable needle, one small crochet hook.

TENSION

Measured over st st, using 3.25mm needles: 24 sts = 10cm.

MATERIALS

Rowan Glace Cotton in Harebell blue: 700g.
Pendant beads: 180.
4 small glass buttons.

BACK AND FRONT

(Worked identically)
Using 3.25mm needles cast on 145 sts.
Row 1 (RS): P3, * p6, (k1 yo k1 yo k1 into next st – known as 'M5'), p7, rep from * to last 2 sts, p2.
Row 2: K2, * k7, p5, k6, rep from * to last 3 sts, k3.
Row 3: P3, * p6, k5, p7, rep from * to last 2 sts, p2.
Row 4: Rep row 2.
Row 5: P3, * p6, sl 1, k1, psso, k1, k2 tog, p7, rep from * to last 2 sts, p2.
Row 6: K2, * k7, p3, k6, rep from * to last 3 sts, k3.
Row 7: P3, * p6, put RH needle point into 2nd st on LH needle as if to k2 tog but slip them, k1, and then pass 2 sl sts over, p7, rep from * to last 2 sts, p2.
Row 8: K2, * k7, p1, k6, rep from * to last 3 sts, k3.
Row 9: P3, * p6, k1tbl and then k1 into same st before slipping off LH needle, now lift the visible strand between these 2 newly made sts with the LH needle and k1tbl (known as M3), p7, rep from * to last 2 sts, p2.
Row 10: K9, p3, k6, * p1, k6, p3, k6, rep from * to last 3 sts, k3.
Row 11: P3, * p6, k1, M3, k1, p6, k1tbl, rep from *, working the last repeat as p6, k1, M3, k1, p to end.
Row 12: K9, p2, k1, p2, k6, * p1, k6, p2, k1, p2, k6, rep from * working the last repeat p1, k6, p2, k1, p2,

k to end.
Row 13: P3, * p5, CB1, k2, p1 from CN, p1, CF2, p1, k2 from CN, p5, k1 tbl, rep from *, working last repeat as p5, CB1, k2, p1 from CN, p1, CF2, p1, k2 from CN, p to end.
Row 14: K7, CF1, p2, k1 from CN, k3, CB2, k1, p2 from CN, k4, * p1, k4, CF1, p2; k1 from CN, k3, CB2, k1, p2 from CN, k4, rep from * to last 3 sts, k3.
Row 15: P3, * p3, CB1, k2, p1 from CN, p5, CF2, p1, k2 from CN, p3, k1 tbl, rep from * working last repeat as p3, CB1, k2, p1 from CN, p5, CF2, p1, k2 from CN, p to end.
Row 16: K5, CF1, p2, k1 from CN, k7, CB2, k1, p2 from CN, k2, * p1, k2, CF1, p2, k1 from CN, k7, CB2, k1, p2 from CN, k2, rep from * to last 3 sts, k3.
Row 17: P3, * p1, CB1, k2, p1 from CN, p9, CF2, p1, k2 from CN, p1, k1 tbl, rep from *, working last rep as p1, CB1, k2, p1 from CN, p9, CF2, p1, k2 from CN, p to end.
Row 18: K3, CF1, p2, k1 from CN, k11, CB2, k1, p2 from CN, * p1, CF1, p2, k1 from CN, k11, CB2, k1, p2 from CN, rep from * to last 3 sts, k3.
Row 19: P2, k3 tog, * p13, k1, sl 1, k2 tog, psso, k1, rep from * to end.
Row 20: K16, * p2 tog, return this st to the LH needle and lift the next st over it, finally returning the result to the RH needle, k13, rep from * to last 3 sts, k3.
These 20 rows form the pattern. Work 7 patts in all.

Shape neck
Next row: Patt 53, cast off 39, patt to end.
Cont with this set of sts, leaving others on a holder.
Dec 1 st at neck edge on every row for 7 more rows.
Row 9: Dec 1 st at the neck edge but do not work the increases in the patt, k these sts instead.
Row 10: Work in reverse st st, dec 1 st at neck edge as before (44 sts). Leave sts on a holder. Return to first

set of sts, join yarn in at neck edge and work to match first side. Leave sts on a spare needle.

SLEEVES

Using 3.25mm needles cast on 47 sts and work in pattern as for body, inc 1 st each end of every 4th row. Work new sts into pattern, remembering to make allowance for the selvedge sts which aren't, strictly speaking, part of the pattern. When you have 103 sts on the needle work straight until the 10th row of the 7th patt rep has been completed. Cast off loosely.

CUFFS

Using 3.25mm needles, cast on 2 sts.
** *Row 1:* Knit.
Row 2: K1, M1 by knitting into strand between sts, k to end.
Keep rep these 2 rows until there are 10 sts on the needle.
Next row: Knit.
Next row: K1, k2 tog, k to end.

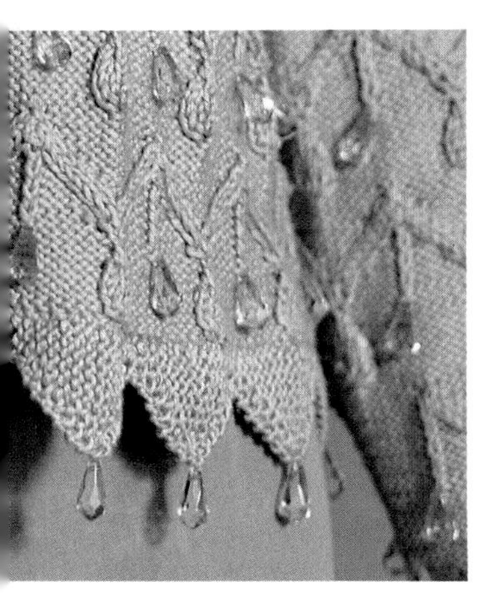

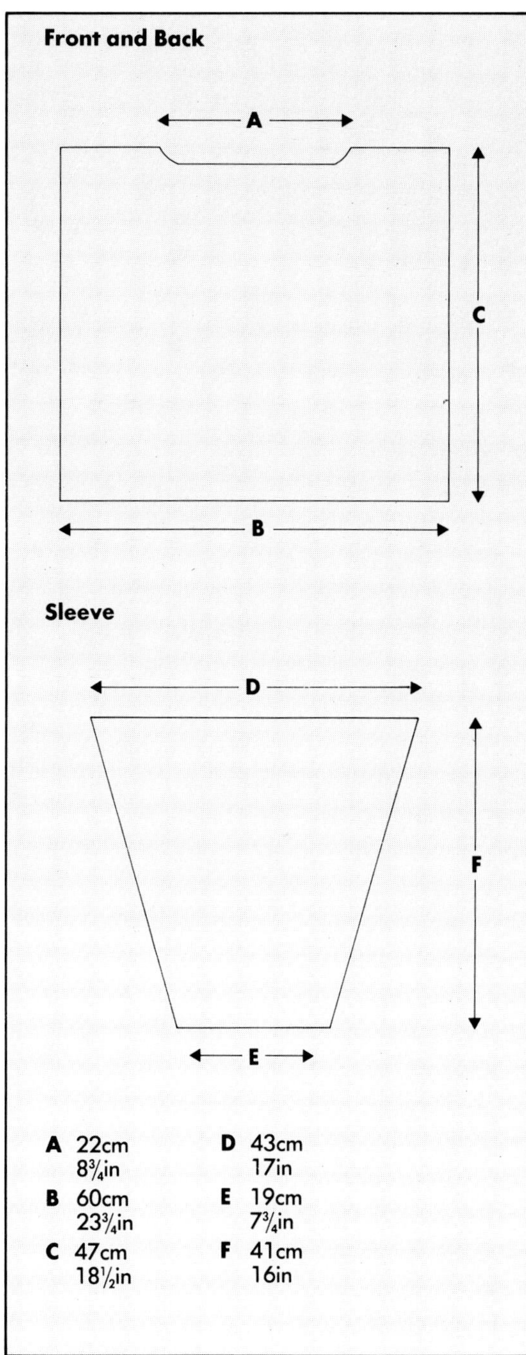

Keep rep these 2 rows until 2 sts remain **.
Rep from ** to ** twice more. Cast off.

HEM BORDER

As for cuff but rep from ** to ** 20 times in all before casting off.

COLLAR

As for cuff but rep ** to ** 10 times in all before casting off.

MAKING UP

Knit both shoulder seams tog on inside of work. Open out work and pin sleeves to body whilst flat, allowing them to find their own depth. Do not bunch into an 'artificial' armhole. Attach with a narrow backstitch. Only now join side seams with a narrow backstitch and join sleeve seams similarly but leaving the first 7cm open to form the cuff opening.

Attach the cuff edging with a flat seam. Crochet a single chain around cuff opening, making two small button loops – one right at the very cuff edge and the other approx 3cm up from first. Attach hem border with a flat seam, lining up the points of the edging with the points made in the pattern.

Join the cast on and cast off edges of the collar tog and line this little seam up with the centre back neck. Attach to neck with a flat seam on inside of neck so that the collar points stand up.

Sew buttons to cuffs and pendant beads to the points in the pattern and the hem points, as shown in close up.

A paisley design, which uses the rich tones of antique shawls as an inspiration, is worked all over this loose-fitting sweater.

perfect

. . *paisley*

NEEDLES

One pair each 3mm and 3.75mm.

TENSION

Measured over pattern using 3.75mm needles: 28sts = 10cm.

NB Use separate balls of chenille for each paisley area, carrying the two silk/wool colours behind and weaving approx every 4 sts.

MATERIALS

Rowan silk/cotton and Rowan fine chenille are used.

Colourway 1

Base: Silk/wool colour no 913: 450/500g.
Outlines: Silk/wool colour no 922: 200/250g.
Paisleys (A and B): Fine chenille plum and lacquer: 50g each colour.

Colourway 2

Swap the following:
Base: Colour no 921.
Paisleys (A and B): Plum and seville.

BACK

Using 3mm needles and base colour, cast on 160/180 sts.

Row 1: K1, p1, rep from * to end.

Keep rep this row to form single rib until it measures 5cm, ending with a RS row. Purl the next row, inc 1 st each end of row (162/182 sts). Change to 3.75mm needles and start working from graph overleaf but keeping the first and last st in base colour as a selvedge throughout (these sts are not marked on graph). Alternate the chenille colours of A + B on each repeat. The graph fits 4/4.5 times across the row. When 2.5 repeats have been worked in depth leave sts on a spare needle.

FRONT

As for back, until row 10 of the third rep.

Shape neck

Next row: Patt 70/80, cast off 22, patt to end. Cont with this set of sts, leaving others on a holder. Dec 1 st at neck edge on every row until 55/65 sts remain. Now work straight until the 32 rows of the half patt are complete. Leave sts on a holder. Return to other side of neck, join yarn in at neck edge and work to match first side. Leave sts on a spare needle.

SLEEVES

Using 3mm needles and base colour, cast on 60/66 sts. Work in single rib for 6/7cm, ending with a RS row. Purl the next row, inc into every 3rd/4th st (80/82 sts). Now change to 3.75mm needles and work graph and selvedge sts as on body, inc 1 st each end of first and every following 4th row until there are 122 sts. **NB** Work each new st, first as a selvedge and then, as the next increase is worked, into pattern. Work straight until 1.5 reps of the pattern are complete. Cast off loosely.

NECKBAND

First knit the right shoulder seam tog on the inside of the work.

Using base colour, 3mm needles and with RS facing, knit up 21 sts down the left side of neck, 22 across front, 21 up other side of neck and then knit 52 centre back neck sts on to the needle (116 sts). Knit the first row and then work in single rib for 7cm. Leave sts on a thread.

MAKING UP

Knit 2nd shoulder seam tog and join neckband edges with a flat seam. Fold neckband in half, in on itself, and slip st down to the first knit row of the band, slipping the sts off of the thread one at a time.

NB Do not twist the band, keep each st at right angles to the fold line.

Open out work and pin sleeves into position, letting them find their own depth. Do not bunch them into an 'artificial' armhole. Attach using a narrow backstitch (try to just take in the selvedge st as a seam allowance). Only now join side and sleeve seams using a flat seam over ribs and a narrow backstitch over pattern.

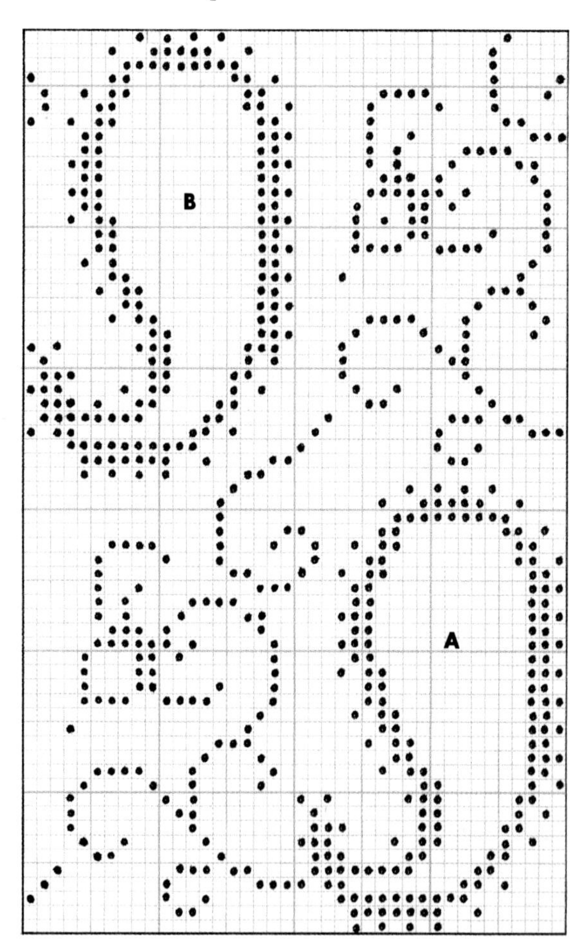

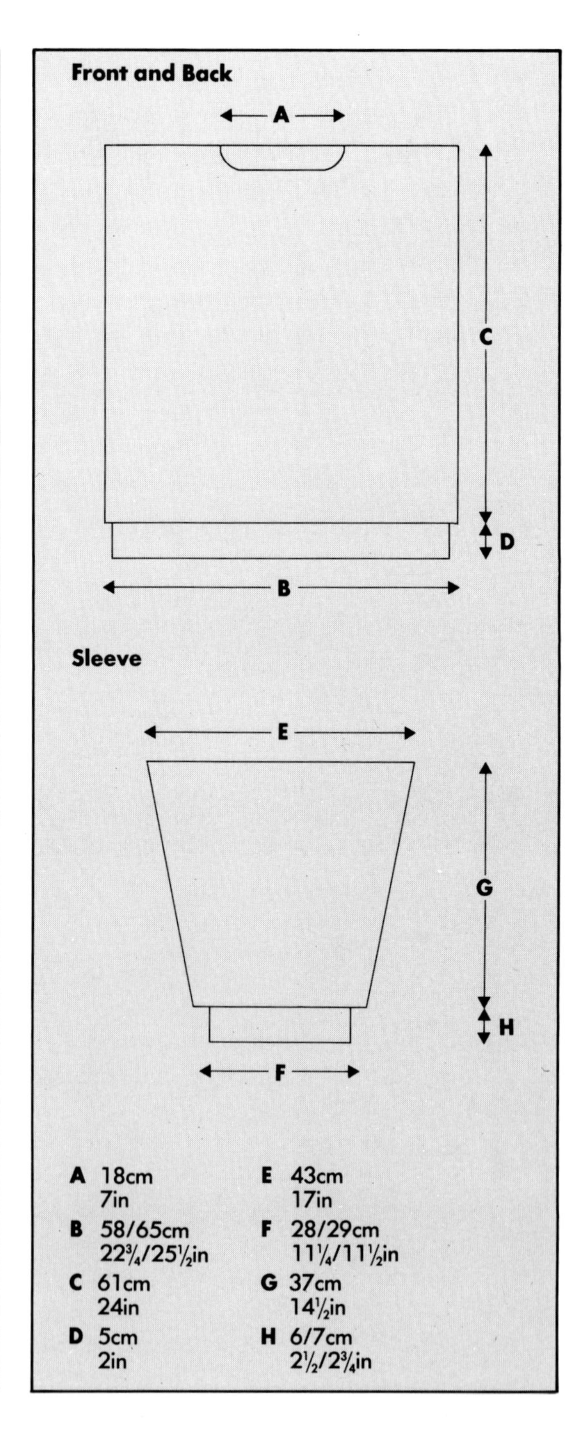

A plunging 'V' neck sweater which makes the most of the unadulterated luxury of pure white cashmere. A trail of beads enhances the design.

creme de . . *la creme*

NEEDLES

One pair each 3.25mm and 2.75mm.

TENSION

Measured over st st using 3.25mm needles:
28 sts = 10cm.

MATERIALS

Jaeger Cashmere: 325/350g.
Beading: 4 strings of small beads, approx 65cm each, plus occasional beads according to preference.

BACK

Using 2.75mm needles, cast on 144/150 sts.
Row 1 (RS): * K1 tbl, p1, rep from * to end.
Row 2: * K1, p1, rep from * to end.
Keep rep these 2 rows to form single twisted rib for 6cm. Now change to 3.25mm needles and cont in st st. When work measures 39/40cm:

Shape armholes
Dec 1 st at each end of every row until 120/126 sts remain. Now work straight until work measures 60/

62cm, ending with a RS row. Leave sts on a spare needle.

FRONT

As for back until work measures 32/34cm from beg, ending with a RS row.

Divide for neck

Next row: P72/75, turn work, leaving remaining sts on a holder.

Row 1: K2, k2 tog tbl, k to end.

Rep this dec row on the 3rd and then every following 4th row. Meanwhile when work measures 39/40cm:

Shape armholes

(Cont to shape neck as before)

Dec 1 st at armhole edge on every row until 12 decs have been worked. Now work this edge straight and cont to shape neck until 35/38 sts remain. Work straight until front matches back. Leave sts on a holder. Return to other side of neck and join yarn in at neck edge, purl the first row and then shape to match first side but working 'k2 tog' instead of 'k2 tog tbl'. Work until this side matches back. Leave sts on the needle.

Now knit the right shoulder seam tog on inside of work. Leave remaining sts on a holder.

SLEEVES

Using 2.75mm needles, cast on 50/54 sts and work in single twisted rib for 6cm. Change to 3.25mm needles and cont in st st, inc 4 sts evenly across the first row

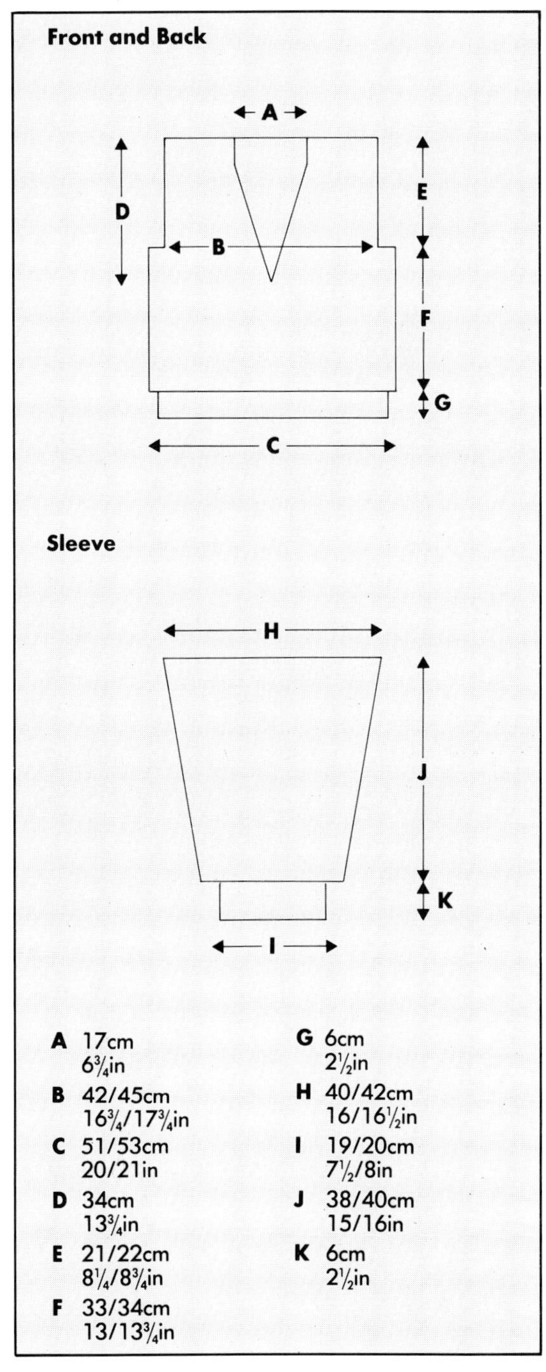

(54/58 sts). Now inc 1 st each end of next and every following 4th row until there are 114/118 sts. Work straight until sleeve measures 44/46cm.

Shape sleeve head

Dec 1 st each end of every row until 92/96 sts remain. Cast off loosely.

NECKBAND

Using 2.75mm needles and with RS facing, knit up 106 sts down left side, make a central st though the strand where the sts were divided, knit up 106 sts from the other side and then knit across the 50 centre back neck sts (263 sts).

Row 1: K1, * p1, k1, rep from * to 3 sts before the central st, k3 tog, p the central st, k3 tog, rib to end.

Row 2: K1 tbl, * p1, k1, rep from * to 3 sts before central st, p3 tog tbl, k-b the central st, p3 tog, work in twisted rib to end.

Cont as set in twisted rib with the central st remaining in st st (k-b on RS rows), with a double dec worked either side.

When band is 2cm deep, cast off in rib, working the decs, as before.

MAKING UP

Knit second shoulder seam tog and join neckband edges with a flat seam.

Position beads as shown in close up and stitch into position using sewing thread rather than yarn.

Join side and sleeve seams with a flat seam over ribs, a narrow backstitch over st st. Set sleeves in, pin and join with a narrow backstitch.

A boxeỳ evening jacket, studded with costume jewellery, worked in a deep texture stitch using chenille to create an impression of quilted velvet.

black . . *velvet*

NEEDLES

One pair of 4mm.

TENSION

To measure tension cast on 19 sts and work the 20 row pattern before casting off loosely. Measure this piece from selvedge to selvedge at the widest part, on the RS of work and without applying any pressure. It should measure 10cm.

MATERIALS

Jaeger Chenille in black: 550g.
175 'gem' stones with holes for sewing.

BACK

Using 4mm needles, cast on 91 sts and work in pattern:

Row 1 (RS): K1, * p3, k11, p3, k1, rep from * to end.
Row 2: P1, * lift thread between st just worked and next st and purl into back of it (known as M1), k3, p2 tog, p7, p2 tog b, k3, M1, p1, rep from * to end.
Row 3: K2, * p3, k9, p3, k3, rep from *, ending k2.
Row 4: P2, * M1, k3, p2 tog, p5, p2 tog b, k3, M1, p3, rep from * ending p2.
Row 5: K3, * p3, k7, p3, k5, rep from *, ending k3.
Row 6: P3, * M1, k3, p2 tog, p3, p2 tog b, k3, M1, p5, rep from * ending p3.
Row 7: K4, * p3, k5, p3, k7, rep from *, ending k4.
Row 8: P4, * M1, k3, p2 tog, p1, p2 tog b, k3, M1, p7, rep from *, ending p4.
Row 9: K5, * p3, k3, p3, k9, rep from *, ending k5.
Row 10: P5, * M1, k3, p3 tog, k3, M1, p9, rep from *, ending p5.
Row 11: K6, * p3, k1, p3, k11, rep from *, ending k6.
Row 12: P4, * p2 tog b, k3, M1, p1, M1, k3, p2 tog, p7, rep from *, ending p4.
Row 13: K5, * p3, k3, p3, k9, rep from *, ending k5.
Row 14: P3, * p2 tog b, k3, M1, p3, M1, k3, p2 tog, p5,

rep from *, ending p3.
Row 15: K4, * p3, k5, p3, k7, rep from *, ending k4.
Row 16: P2, * p2 tog b, k3, M1, p5, M1, k3, p2 tog, p3, rep from *, ending p2.
Row 17: K3, * p3, k7, p3, k5, rep from * ending k3.
Row 18: P1, * p2 tog b, k3, M1, p7, M1, k3, p2 tog, p1, rep from * to end.
Row 19: K2, * p3, k9, p3, k3, rep from *, ending k2.
Row 20: P2 tog b, * k3, M1, p9, M1, k3, p3 tog, rep from * ending with p2 tog (instead of p3 tog).
These 20 rows form the pattern. Keep rep throughout unless otherwise instructed. When pattern has been worked 4 times in all:

Shape armholes
(Keeping in pattern as you go)
Cast off 3 sts at beg of next 2 rows. Now dec 1 st at each end of every row until 79 sts remain. Now dec 1 st at each end of every alt row until 73 sts remain. Work straight until 7 patt reps have been worked. Leave sts on a holder.

RIGHT FRONT

Using 4mm needles, cast on 55 sts. Work in pattern as for back until 4 patt reps have been worked.

Shape armhole
(Cont in patt)
Next WS row: Cast off 3 sts, patt to end. Now dec 1 st at armhole edge on every row until 49 sts remain and then dec 1 st at this edge on every alt row until 46 sts remain. Work straight until 6 reps of patt have been completed.

Shape neck
(Cont in patt)
Next RS row: Firmly cast off 9 sts, patt to end. Now

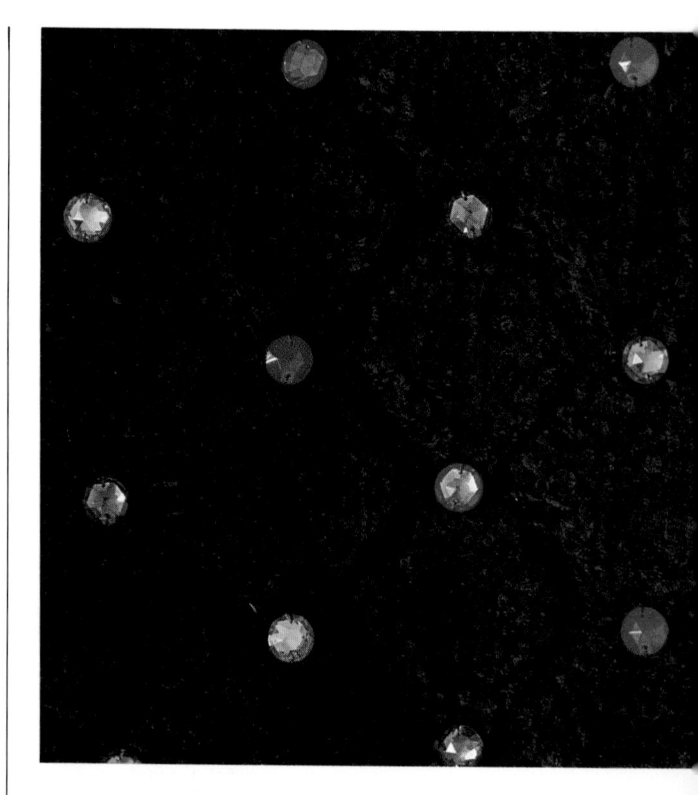

dec 1 st at neck edge on every row until 21 sts remain. Work straight until front matches back.

LEFT FRONT

As for right front, reversing out shapings.

SLEEVES

Using 4mm needles, cast on 37 sts. Work in patt as for back, inc 1 st each end of every 6th row, keeping new sts in patt as you go, until there are 73 sts. Now work straight until 6 patt reps have been worked.

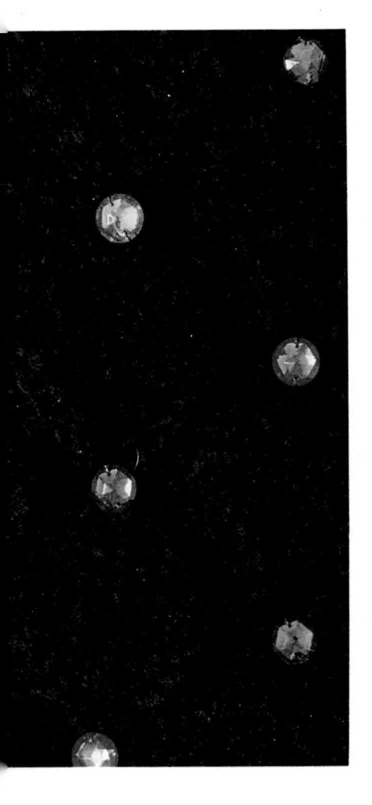

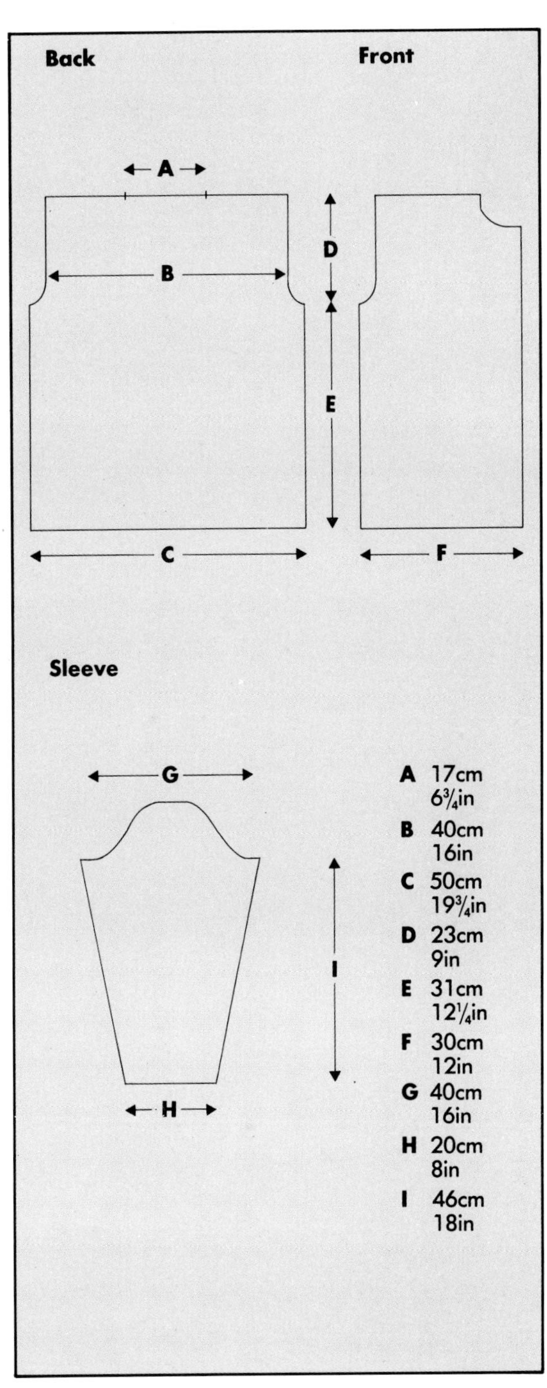

special *effect*

BLOCKING

Carefully pin the section of work (the illustration shows a pocket flap) to required shape. Hold a steam iron a few centimetres above the knitting

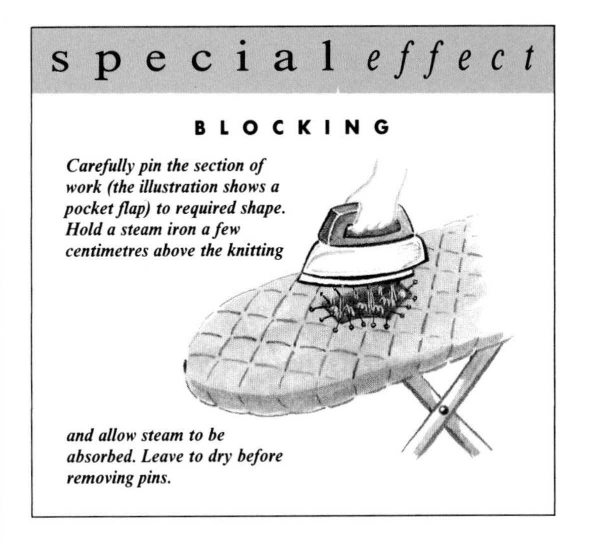

and allow steam to be absorbed. Leave to dry before removing pins.

Shape sleeve head

Cast off 3 sts at beg of next 2 rows. Now dec 1 st each end of every row until 55 sts remain. Now dec 1 st each end of every alt row until 23 sts remain and 2 patt reps have been worked since starting the sleeve head shaping. Cont in rev st st, casting off 5 sts at beg of next 2 rows. Cast off remaining 13 sts.

MAKING UP

Knit first shoulder seam tog on inside of work, firmly cast off 31 sts for back neck and then knit other shoulder seam tog

Block front edges in a straight line and lightly steam (see diagram above).

Attach gemstones while garment is still in pieces for easy access. Position them at stitch 'intersections', as shown in close up. Use sewing thread to attach rather than chenille. Join side and sleeve seams with a flat seam. Set sleeves in, carefully pinning and then joining with a narrow backstitch.

A multi-coloured sweater which uses the entrelac method of knitting so that only one colour at a time is worked.

a u t u m n *p a t c h w o r k*

NEEDLES

One pair each 3.25mm and 3.75mm needles.

TENSION

Using 3.75mm needles and measured over st st: 24 sts = 10cm.

MATERIALS

In Rowan light-weight DK: 100g each of the 8 shades. A = 45, B = 81, C = 09, D = 26, E = 407, F = 78, G = 77, H = 404.

NB Each triangle or rectangle is worked in a different colour. The colour sequence goes loosely in alphabetical order but if a colour is falling next to itself or is lining up too symetrically, jump one or two colours to achieve a random effect. (See diagram overleaf.)

BACK AND FRONT

(Worked identically)
Using A and 3.75mm needles, cast on 112 sts.

Form base triangles
Row 1 (WS): P2, turn.
Row 2: K2, turn.
Row 3: P3 (purling the extra st from the LH needle), turn.
Row 4: K3, turn.
Row 5: P4, turn.
Row 6: K4, turn.
Cont as set, adding an extra st on every purl row until there are 8 sts on the RH needle, ending with a purl row. This forms one triangle. Work 13 more in the same way so that all 112 sts are now on the RH needle.

special *effect*

ENTRELAC

The arrows indicate the direction in which each triangle or rectangle is knitted.

***** Work selvedge triangle***

Row 1: K2, turn.
Row 2: P2, turn.
Row 3: Inc into the first st, sl 1, k1, psso, turn.
Row 4: P3, turn.
Row 5: K1, inc into next st, sl 1, k1, psso, turn.
Row 6: P4, turn.
Row 7: K1, inc into next st, k1, sl 1, psso, turn.
Row 8: P5, turn.
Row 9: K1, inc into next st, k2, sl 1, k1, psso, turn.
Cont as set, inc into the 2nd st on every k row until there are 8 sts, ending with a k row.

Work the first rectangle

This being knitted up from the second side of the first base triangle (see diagram above for direction of knitting).
Knit up 8 sts along this edge, working from top to bottom with the RS facing.
Row 1: P8, turn.
Row 2: K7, sl 1, k next st from LH needle, psso, turn.
Keep rep these last 2 rows until all the sts from the first side of the second triangle have been incorporated. This completes the first rectangle. Work a rectangle from the 10 following triangles and then from the second side of the last triangle form a selvedge triangle.

Selvedge triangle

Knit up 8 sts as from the previous triangles.
Row 1: P2 tog, p6, turn.
Row 2: K7.
Row 3: P2 tog, p5, turn.
Cont as set, until 1 st remains, fasten off.
Another line of rectangles is now worked in the opposite direction, starting by knitting up 8 sts from bottom to top along the inner edge of the selvedge triangle just worked, RS facing.
Row 1: P7, p2 tog (1 st from triangle, 1 st from rectangle).
Row 2: K8.
Keep rep last 2 rows until all the sts from the rectangle have been incorporated. Work remaining rectangles as set, finishing by incorporating the sts from the selvedge triangle at the end. ** Rep from ** to ** 8 times more. Now finish with a straight edge by forming a row of triangles.
Row 1: K2, turn.
Row 2: P2, turn.
Row 3: Inc into first st, sl 1, k1, psso, turn.
Row 4: P3, turn.
Row 5: K1, inc into next st, sl 1, k1, psso, turn.
Row 6: P4, turn.
Row 7: K1, inc into next st, k1, sl 1, k1, psso, turn.
Row 8: P5, turn.
Row 9: K2 tog, k2, sl 1, k1, psso, turn.
Row 10: P4, turn.
Row 11: K2 tog, k1, sl 1, k1, psso, turn.
Row 12: P3, turn.
Row 13: K2 tog, sl 1, k1, psso, turn.
Row 14: P2 tog, turn. Slip this st onto RH needle and then knit up 8 sts along the second side of the first rectangle from top to bottom, RS facing.
Row 1: P7, p2 tog.
Row 2: Sl 1, k1, psso, k5, sl 1, k1 (from next rectangle), psso, turn.

Row 3: P7.
Row 4: Sl 1, k1, psso, k4, sl 1, k1, psso, turn.
Row 5: P6.
Cont as set until you are purling 2 sts only.
Next row: K1, sl 1, k1, psso, k1, turn.
Next row: Sl 1, p2 tog, psso.
Work from the next 8 rectangles in the same manner and finish with another triangle, first knitting up 8 sts from the last rectangle, as before.
Row 1: P7, p2 tog.
Row 2: Sl 1, k1, psso, k4, k2 tog.
Row 3: P6.
Row 4: Sl 1, k1, psso, k2, k2 tog.
Row 5: P4.
Row 6: Sl 1, k1, psso, k2 tog.
Row 7: P2.
Row 8: K2 tog and fasten off.

SLEEVES

Using A and 3.25mm needles, cast on 64 sts.
Row 1: * K2, p2, rep from * to end.
Keep rep this row to form double rib, working 2 rows in each colour, in sequence, then 2 rows in A. Change to 3.75mm needles and form 8 base triangles. Work from ** to ** 7 times in all. Finish with a row of triangles as for top of back.

NECKBAND

Using 3.25 needles and A, cast on 148 sts and work in double rib in colour sequence as for cuffs. Cast off in rib.

MAKING UP

Join shoulder seams with a flat seam, leaving a 25cm neck opening. Open out front and back. Pin sleeves into position taking great care to flatten out so that the armhole is deep enough either side of shoulder seam. Sew side and sleeve seams with a flat seam over the ribs and a very narrow backstitch over the pattern.

Join the edges of the neckband to form a circle and then attach to the neckline by the cast on edge using a flat seam.

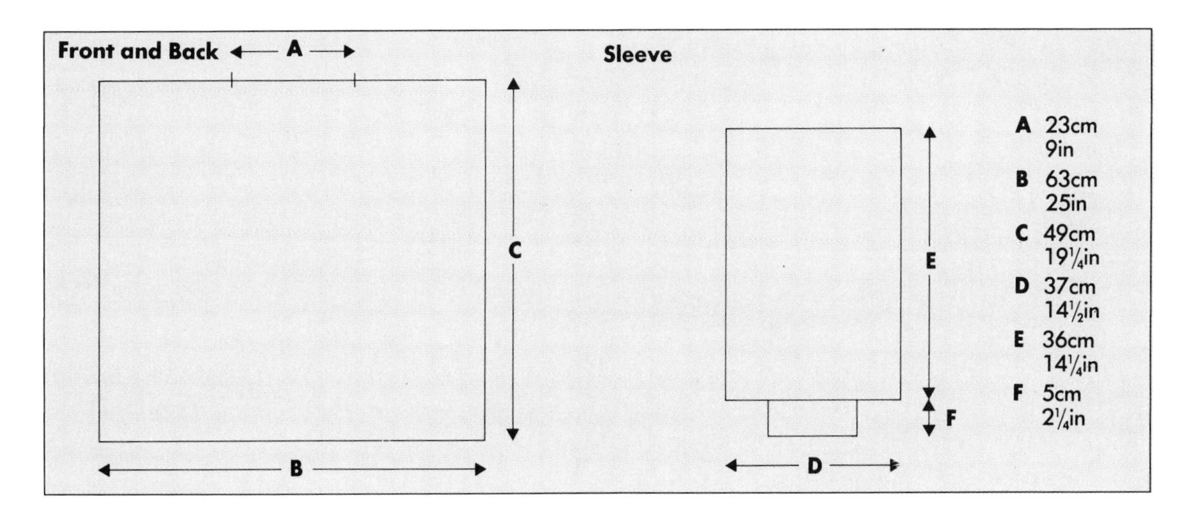

A sumptuous wrap-around mock-fur coat knitted in cream mohair, and with the shawl collar and cuffs trimmed with 'ermine' tails.

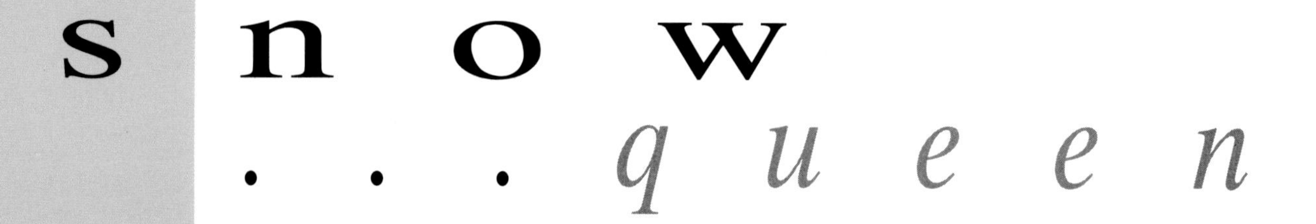

NEEDLES

One pair each 5mm and 4.5mm.

TENSION

Measured over st st, using 5mm needles:
18 sts = 10cm.

MATERIALS

Paton's Mohair in Cream: 1050g; Black (used for tails only): 50g.
One pair of large raglan shoulder pads.

BACK

Using 4.5mm needles, cast on 116 sts. Knit every row (garter st) for 3cm. Change to 5mm needles and cont in st st from now on. Work until it measures 78cm from beg, ending with a WS row.

Shape raglan
Cast off 2 sts at beg of next 2 rows.
Next row: K2, sl 1, k1, psso, k to last 4 sts, k2 tog, k2.
Row 2: Purl.
Keep rep these 2 rows until 54 sts remain. Now dec 1 st at each end of every row until 20 sts remain. Cast off.

LEFT FRONT

Using 4.5mm needles, cast on 58 sts and work in garter st for 3cm. Change to 5mm needles and cont in st st until work measures 68cm, ending with a RS row.

Shape neck
Dec 1 st at neck edge on next and every following 8th row until 10 decs have been worked at this edge. At the same time when work measures 78cm, ending with a WS row

Shape raglan

Next row: Cast off 2 sts, k to end.

Now dec 1 st at raglan edge on every alt row whilst shaping neck as before. When 10 decs have been worked at neck edge work this edge straight whilst cont to dec on every alt row at raglan edge until 18 sts remain. Now dec 1 st on every row at this edge until 2 sts remain. Work 2 tog and fasten off.

RIGHT FRONT

As for left front, reversing out the shapings.

SLEEVES

Using 4.5mm needles, cast on 66 sts and work in garter st for 12cm. Change to 5mm needles and work in st st. When work measures 24cm from beg start to inc 1 st each end of next and every following 5th row until there are 88 sts. Work straight until sleeve measures 48cm, ending with a WS row.

Shape raglan

Cast off 2 sts at beg of next 2 rows.

Next row: K2, sl 1, k1, psso, k to last 4 sts, k2 tog, k2.

Row 2: Purl.

Keep rep last 2 rows until 8 sts remain. Cast off.

RIGHT COLLAR

Using 4.5mm needles, cast on 4 sts and work in garter st for 10 rows (cont in garter st throughout).

Next (RS) row: K1, inc 1 (by knitting into the st on the row below the next st and then that st itself), inc 1, k1.

Knit 7 rows straight.

Next row: K2, (inc 1) twice, k2.

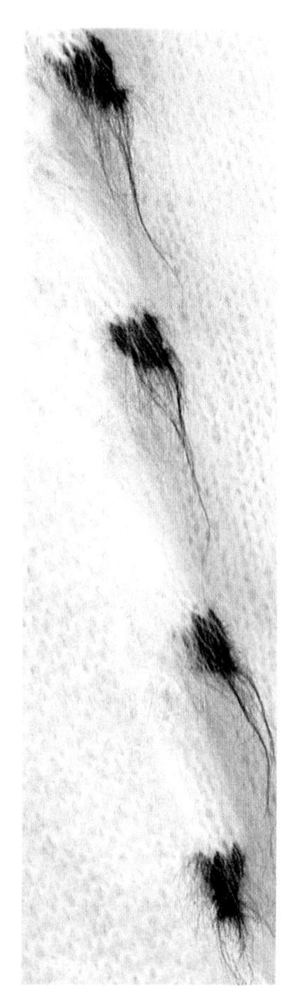

Work 7 rows straight.
Next row: K2, inc 1, k to last 2 sts, inc 1, k1.
Rep the last 8 rows until there are 70 sts on the needle.
* *Next WS row:* K 40, turn and k to end. *
Work 10 rows straight and then rep the turning row from * to *. Work straight until it measures 120cm from beg on the side with the fewest rows. Leave sts on a spare needle.

LEFT COLLAR

As for right, but work the turning rows starting on the RS of work. Knit the two collar pieces tog.

TAILS

(34 to be worked in all)
Using 4.5mm needles and cream, cast on 2 sts and work in st st, inc 1 st at end of next 2 rows (4 sts), now work straight until it's 6cm from beg. Change to black, work 1 row straight and then cont in st st, dec 1 st at beg of each row until 2 sts remain. Work 2 tog and fasten off.

MAKING UP

Join all seams with a flat seam, remembering that the garter st part of the sleeve is a turn back cuff so the seam should be worked on the RS and then the WS for the rest of the sleeve. Attach collar to neck by the edge which has the fewest rows. Place collar seam at the exact centre back neck and the cast on edges flush with the hemline. Divide collar and coat edges into sections and pin carefully so that the collar is distributed evenly and the coat fronts will hang correctly.

Attach tails to collar edge as shown in close up.

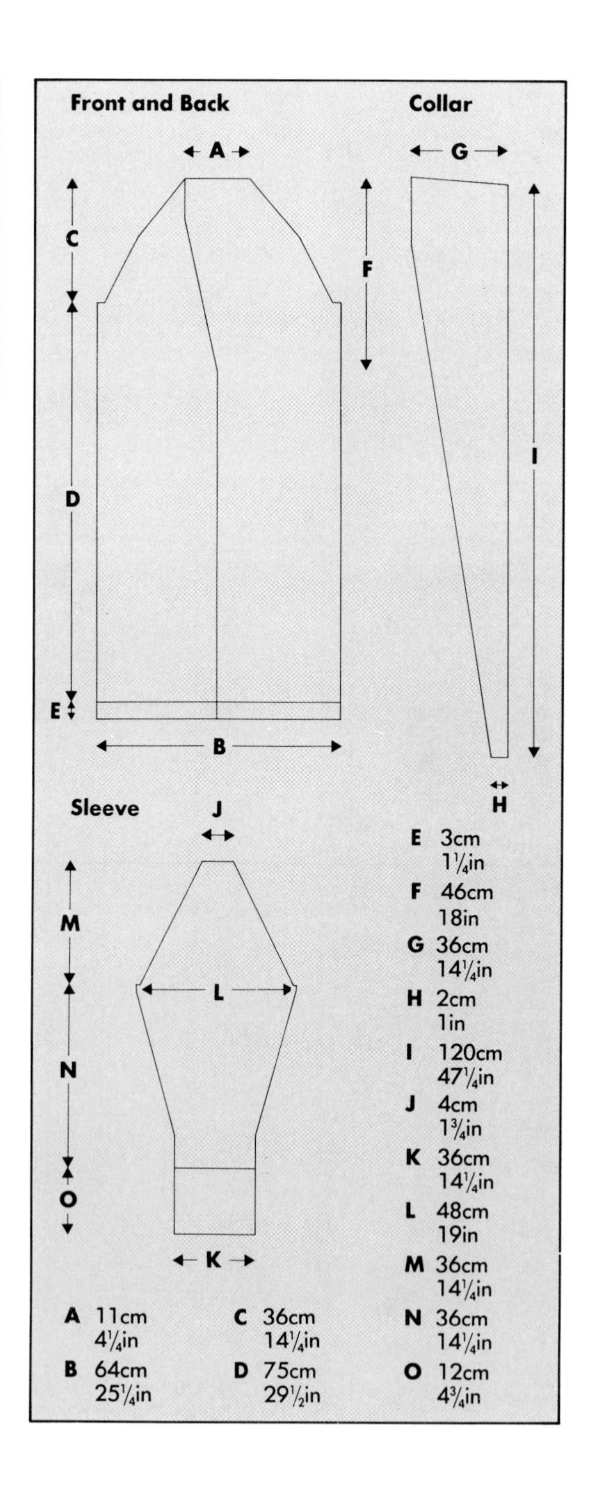

NEEDLE EQUIVALENT CHART

Old U.K.	Metric	American
14	2mm	0
13	2.25mm	1
12	2.75mm	2
11	3mm	2
10	3.25mm	3
-	-	4
9	3.75	5
8	4mm	6
7	4.5mm	7
6	5mm	8
5	5.5mm	9
4	6mm	10
3	6.5mm	10½
2	7mm	-
1	7.5mm	-
0	8mm	11
00	9mm	13
000	10mm	15

QUICK CONVERSION CHART

cm	in
1	⅜
5	2
10	4
15	6
20	8
25	10
30	12
35	14
40	16
45	18
50	20
55	22
60	24
65	26
70	28
75	30
80	32
85	34
90	36
95	38
100	39½

NOTES FOR NORTH AMERICAN READERS

Knitting is becoming more and more international; and knitters, especially in the larger towns and cities, have access to many yarns and patterns from abroad. American and Canadian readers should have no trouble using the patterns in this book. However, some North American readers may occasionally need to refer to the information given here.

METRIC MEASUREMENTS

In this book metric measurements are used within the pattern instructions, with both metric and imperial (U.S. standard) given in the diagrams. If you are not familiar with metric measurements, there is no need to be wary of them. They are actually very easy to use, because they are based on the decimal system.

If you have not already got a tape measure with both metric and imperial/standard measurements, you should buy one; the kind with both systems on the same side is most useful when you are just learning to use metric.

The basic linear metric units are:

millimetre/(mm) = approximately $\frac{1}{25}$ inch
centimetre (cm: 10mm) = approximately ⅜ inch
metre (m: 100cm) = approximately 39½ inches

To find the number of inches in a metric measurement, divide the number of centimetres by 2.54. Thus, 30cm = 11.8 inches (normally rounded up to 12). (The conversion chart (left) gives you a quick guide.)

To convert metres into yards: multiply the number of metres by 1.09. Thus, 4.5 metres = 4.9 yards (normally rounded up to 5 yards).

Metric weight measurements The smallest metric unit of weight (and the only one used in knitting patterns) is the gram (g). There are approximately 28 grams to the ounce, so a 50-gram ball of yarn weighs slightly less than 2 ounces.

To convert gram measurements accurately into ounces, divide by 28.35. Thus, 600g of yarn = 21.16 ounces. To be on the safe side, round this up to 22, if buying yarn.

A word of caution Whenever you are working on a project that involves measurements, choose one system or the other and then *stick to it*. Confusion will result if you jump from one to the other.

BUYING YARNS

Specific yarns are recommended for the garments in this book. All of these yarns are currently available in the United States and Canada, as well as Britain. For the address of the nearest retailer (or a mail-order supplier) of a particular yarn, contact the manufacturer or distributer (see page 96).

Substituting yarns It is always best to use the recommended yarn for a pattern. This is especially true in the case of a textured or novelty yarn, for the design has been created to display that yarn's particular qualities. If, however, you are unable to obtain the recommended yarn, you may be able to substitute another – provided you can obtain the specified gauge or tension. Buy one ball of the yarn, and knit up a gauge swatch using the recommended needles. Change needles if necessary until you obtain the correct gauge.

Note, however, that even though you may be able, by changing needles, to obtain the required gauge, the fabric produced may be unattractively stiff or flimsy if the substitute yarn is thicker or thinner, respectively, than the recommended one. For example, it is not a good idea to substitute an American knitting worsted for a British or Continental double knitting yarn (the closest equivalent), because the former is noticeably thicker than the latter. This is generally true of all the main categories of smooth yarn: the European type is generally finer than its closest American equivalent.

A sales assistant in a good yarn shop should be able to advise you on substituting yarns and to calculate the amount of yarn you will need.

NEEDLE EQUIVALENT CHART

Metric needle sizes have been specified for the patterns in this book. If your needles are sized according to the American or the old U.K. systems, you can find the corresponding size in the chart (left). Note, however, that many of the equivalents are approximate.

YARN SUPPLIERS

All the yarns in this book should be readily obtainable from good yarn shops. If you are having difficulty finding a yarn please contact the spinners direct at the address given below.

JAEGER HANDKNITTING AND PATONS

United Kingdom McMullen Road, Darlington, Co. Durham DL1 1YQ.
Tel: 0325 380123
United States Susan Bates Inc, 212 Middlesex Avenue, Chester, Connecticut 06412.
Tel: 203 526 5381
Canada 1001 Rose Lawn Avenue, Toronto.
Australia 98-91 Peter's Avenue, Mulgrave, Victoria 3170.
New Zealand 263 Ti Rakau Drive, Pakuranga, Auckland.
South Africa 4 Wol Street, Randfontein, Transvaal.

ROWAN YARNS

United Kingdom Rowan Up Country, 6 Market Walk, Holmfirth, West Yorkshire.
Tel: 0484 687803
Mail Order: Access/Visa. Tel: 0484 681881 for list of UK stockists.
United States Westminster Trading Corporation, 5 Northern Boulevard, Amherst, New Hampshire 03031.
Tel: 603 886 5041
Canada Estelle Designs and Sales Ltd, 38 Continental Place, Scarborough, Ontario.
Tel: 416 298 9922
Australia Sunspun Enterprises Pty Ltd, 191 Canterbury Road, Canterbury, 3126 Victoria.
Tel: 03 830 1609
New Zealand Creative Fashion Centre, PO Box 45083, Epuni Railway, Lower Hutt.
Tel: 04 674 085

TWILLEYS

United Kingdom H.G. Twilley Ltd, Roman Mill, Stamford, Lincolnshire PE9 1BG.
Tel: 0780 52661
United States Scotts Woollen Mill, 528 Jefferson Avenue, Bristol, PA 19007.
Tel: 215 788 0459
Canada S.R. Kertzer Ltd, 257 Adelaide Street West, Toronto.
Australia Panda Yarns, 17-27 Brunswick Road, East Brunswick, Victoria 3057.
New Zealand Alliance Textiles International Ltd, 534 Kaikorai Valley Road, Dunedin.

MAIL ORDER

As an alternative to contacting the suppliers direct, The Wool Works, 48 Friar Street, Worcester, WR1 2NA, tel: 0905 29228, offers a mail order service for many of the yarns included in this book. (To supply orders overseas – Mastercard or Visa is required.) For Jaeger and Patons yarn only try The Hand Knitters Guild, 12, The Strand, Cwmbran, Gwent NP44 1PA. For a UK-only service supplying Twilley's yarn write to Rena Wools, PO Box 23, Oakham, Leicestershire LE15 6XJ.
Freephone 0800 626150

ACCESSORIES

For beads, stones, coins try Creative Beadcraft Ltd, (Ells and Farrier), 20 Princes Street, London W.1. For a mail order service write to Denmark Works, Sheepcote Dell Road, Beamond End, Bucks HP7 0RX.
Tel: 0444 715606